Stalwarts of Indian Police

Edited by
Sankar Sen

Stalwarts of Indian Police
Edited by Sankar Sen

© Sankar Sen

First Published 2020
Reprinted 2021

ISBN 978-93-5002-676-2

All rights reserved. No part of this book may be reproduced or transmitted, in any form or by any means, without the prior permission of the Publisher.

Published by
AAKAR BOOKS
28 E Pocket IV, Mayur Vihar Phase I
Delhi 110 091 India
aakarbooks@gmail.com

Laser Typeset at
Arpit Printographers, Delhi

Printed at
Sapra Brothers, Noida

Contents

अजीत डोभाल, कीर्ति चक्र
राष्ट्रीय सुरक्षा सलाहकार
Ajit Doval, KC
National Security Adviser

प्रधान मंत्री कार्यालय
नई दिल्ली–110 011
PRIME MINISTER'S OFFICE
NEW DELHI - 110 011

FOREWORD

India's transition from a colonial rule to a nascent democracy was a tumultuous experiment of history, which with passage of time, we fail to fully appreciate. Centuries of subjugation had led to economic deprivation, social dissonance, ethnic and communal divides with a colonial infrastructure designed to promote interests of the rulers rather than serve the people. Nearly 40% of India was under princely states and was yet to be integrated where the police and civil administration was non-existent or very weak. In those days, few gave India a chance to survive as a united nation given its fault lines. It was hard work and grit of our forbearers, in diverse fields that enabled India to emerge as a powerful nation and vibrant democracy that it is today.

Post-independent India also inherited numerous security challenges. Partition led to large scale exodus of populations marred by widespread communal violence and riots. There were millions of hapless refugees with no shelter, safety or means of livelihood. Within months of gaining its independence, India faced state-sponsored attacks by tribal raiders from Pakistan into Kashmir, a problem that the nation continues to grapple with. Economic inequalities, social conflicts, feudal agrarian sector, illiteracy and depravity created its own tensions impacting on law and order situation.

To cope with all these problems, India had a grossly inadequate police force that was ill-equipped and ill-trained to meet the needs and aspirations of the people of a free democracy. Most of the British officers, manning senior positions in police and intelligence had left the country leaving a leadership void. While the police in British India had a colonial mindset, the police forces from princely states were feudal in their orientation – both unsuitable to meet the requirements of a free and aspirational India.

The police leadership of those early years shouldered these onerous and daunting responsibilities and discharged them well. They could successfully deal with these seemingly insurmountable challenges due to supreme sacrifices made by a large number of police personnel and the exemplary leadership provided by many stalwarts of Indian Police. These leaders were tall men, great visionaries and men of impeccable integrity who built Indian Police with unwavering commitment. They made sterling contributions in their service to the nation.

Most importantly, these Police Stalwarts were harbingers of change with order in challenging times. Even as most post-Colonial States were unable to sustain democracy amidst mounting challenges, they ensured that India's transformation to a modern State was orderly, peaceful and through democratic means.

In the years that followed many new and formidable internal and external security problems raised their ugly head. Left Wing extremism, insurgencies in North East, agrarian agitations, communal riots, linguistic conflicts, etc., are few of them. Soon, organized crimes, with trans-national linkages, emerged as a new threat that included smuggling, gun running, currency counterfeiting, drugs, human trafficking etc. Period of post eighties witnessed emergence of Pak-sponsored terrorism as a major threat. All these were handled by the police forces of the country with high commitment and imaginative leadership. A good number of these problems though still linger on today they have largely been contained within manageable limits.

In this context, this book is a commendable effort by ARSIPSO to spotlight the lives and careers of eighteen legendary leaders of the Police service. Being part of the fraternity of Indian Police, I had the privilege of knowing and working closely with some of these iconic figures. They were instrumental in the transformation of the Police from an institution protecting and promoting colonial interests to a Service meant to secure the lives, liberty and rights of the citizens of a free and democratic country.

These Police leaders provided inspiring leadership in their unique styles and ways and were endowed with multi-faceted personalities. They touched the lives of innumerable men under their command by their human qualities. They also mentored future generations of police leaders.

The riveting narration of facts and anecdotes brought out by the contributors of the articles, who are themselves accomplished and respected Police and Intelligence offices, aptly captures the essence of the contributions made by the Titans of Indian Police. This book besides being a tribute to the Police leaders of yester years will guide present and future generations of Police officers to establish high benchmarks of achievement.

(Ajit Doval)

New Delhi
28 October 2019

Preface

The book *The Stalwarts of Indian Police* is a humble endeavour by the Association of Retired Senior Police Officers (ARSIPSO) to chronicle the work and achievements, trials and tribulations of eighteen outstanding and charismatic Indian police leaders of the country. They were men of shining integrity and unwavering commitment, who inspired and electrified the officers serving under them, and rendered yeoman service for the country in various capacities. They were, to quote John Milton: "Tall men sun crowned, who live above the fog, in public duty, and in private thinking."

Admittedly, a dismaying feature of the police job is that the failures of the police are highlighted but their triumphs and achievements go unheralded. In ARSIPSO, we felt that many of the police stalwarts will remain unknown to the general public and, passed over to the limbo of oblivion, unless their achievements are chronicled objectively, and lessons drawn from them. Moreover, their dedicated service records and superlative standards of excellence could be a source of inspiration to the future generations of police officers.

The contributors of the articles themselves are senior police and intelligence officers, who had the privilege of directly working under the police titans about whom they have written, and witnessed their tireless exertions and dedicated service to the country. The book offers to the readers, a riveting narration of facts, anecdotes and observations on police chiefs, to whom the path of duty was the way to glory.

I express my grateful and appreciative thanks to the contributors of the articles who promptly responded to my request. My sincere thanks also go to Sanjay Sinha, IPS (Retd) for rendering help in collection of photographs, and untangling some administrative problems. I am also grateful to Smt. Gouri Sen for her ungrudging help in editing the pages, and to my Secretary, Dleep Mehta, for typing the manuscripts carefully.

Sankar Sen

1

B.N. Mullick: The Man and His Mission

M.K. Narayanan

Reams have been written about the glory of ancient India, and how it showed the way to the rest of the world in several fields, including intelligence and statecraft. Two of the best known figures of the ancient world, linked to the world of intelligence, were Chanakya of India—350-275 BCE and Sun Tzi of China—544-496

BCE. Machiavelli's *Prince* in the sixteenth century also contained a wealth of information regarding both intelligence and statecraft. Generations of intelligence specialists have honed their skills, studying the works of these great masters, and tried to fashion themselves in the same mould.

The modern world has also produced many outstanding intelligence specialists, though few of them achieved as exalted a status as Chanakya or Sun Tzi. The exploits of Adm. Canaris and Gen. Gehlen of Germany, Alan Dulles and Edgar Hoover of the United States, and a succession of mysterious Cs of UK's MI 6 during the First and Second World Wars, have filled many pages of intelligence history. What was lost sight of is that a host of other intelligence chiefs and specialists, during the nineteenth and twentieth centuries, also contributed in substantial measure to the art and craft of intelligence. Among them was the redoubtable B.N. Mullick.

The British rule in India ushered in an era of intelligence revival, as the British greatly depended on intelligence to keep control over the vast territories they held, many times larger than their own country. Among the stellar leaders of pre-independent India responsible for the rejuvenation of intelligence was Col. Sleeman, who used intelligence to curb the menace of thugs during the mid-nineteenth century. The so-called 'Thuggie Daftar' was the precursor of today's intelligence organizations in India. The Intelligence Bureau, established in 1887—which makes it one of the oldest intelligence organizations in the world—owed its origins to the Sleeman organization. In course of time, the Intelligence Bureau was to spawn many other subsidiary intelligence establishments, centred both in Delhi and in the states. The modern day intelligence apparatus in India is, to an extent, a refined and finessed version of what existed in a small way in the mid-nineteenth and the early twentieth centuries.

Bhola Nath Mullick, one of the most distinguished individuals to adorn the ranks of the Indian police, belonged to its 1927 batch. He was allotted to the Bihar-Orissa Cadre, and served with distinction as Superintendent of Police and Deputy Inspector General of Police, earning several accolades over the years before coming to the Intelligence Bureau as Deputy Director. Under the British rule, the senior hierarchy of the IB was the preserve of British officers, with a sprinkling of Muslim officers in later years. The Hindu and Sikh officers were suspect in the eyes of the British Government, for their presumed sympathy for the nationalist cause.

The first Hindu officer to join the Intelligence Bureau at a senior level prior to independence, was Rameshwar Nath Kao (who much later, became the first head of the Research and Analysis Wing—India's premier external Intelligence Agency). Immediately after independence, the Intelligence Bureau got its first Indian Director, Sanjeevi Pillai. Among the earliest post-independence entrants was M.K. Sinha, IP, who held the rank of Deputy Director. Mr. Sinha, who belonged to the Bihar Cadre and B.N. Mullick were later to exchange places, with Mr. Sinha going back to Bihar and Mr. Mullick replacing him in the Intelligence Bureau.

The initial years of independence were a stormy period for India. The Intelligence Bureau, already saddled with the task of changing its visage from the colonial agency to an intelligence organization of independent India, had to wrestle with a host of problems to safeguard India's new-found independence—from both internal disruptive forces and external enemies. The change over was not an easy one for the Intelligence Bureau. Sanjeevi Pillai, however, performed with conspicuous skill in reshaping the Intelligence Bureau and altering its trajectory. Unfortunately, he fell a victim to intrigue and malice at higher levels, and opted to return to his parent cadre, viz. Madras, as Inspector General of Police. This left a serious void in the Intelligence Bureau at a particularly difficult time.

Legend has it that none of the senior Inspector Generals of Police across the country were keen to take on the responsibility of becoming the Director, Intelligence Bureau, after the treatment meted out to Sanjeevi Pillai. The choice, hence, fell on B.N. Mullick, who had earned the distinction of being one of the most outstanding officers in the police, and the seniormost Deputy Director in the Intelligence Bureau. It was an extraordinary and unusual move, since the Director, Intelligence Bureau is the seniormost police officer in the country, and the post is normally occupied by one of the seniormost Inspectors General of Police. At the time Mullick was anointed (in 1950) as the Director, Intelligence Bureau, he held the rank of Deputy Director in the Intelligence Bureau, equivalent to a Deputy Inspector General of Police.

The decision, however, proved to be a highly propitious one from the point of view of the country's intelligence, and the Intelligence Bureau itself. The nation had a relatively young visionary (Mr. Mullick was about 45 years of age at the time he was appointed), as the Director, one who possessed sterling qualities of head and heart, and capable of completing the blueprint drawn up by the first Indian Director of the nascent (post-independence) Intelligence Bureau. The new Chief also had a reputation for probity, secular values and right conduct. This was indeed most fortunate, as several countries which had gained independence around the same period after World War II, had turned despotic and anti-democratic, with unscrupulous intelligence chiefs supporting despotic heads of state to circumvent democracy and exercise unbridled authority and power.

As the Director, Intelligence Bureau, Mr. Mullick faced several hurdles and took time to formally establish his authority as the intelligence czar. In this, he was greatly helped by the special relationship he could establish with the then Prime Minister, Pandit Jawaharlal Nehru. It was a relationship that endured for almost a decade and a half from 1950 to 1964. Prime Minister Nehru's faith in his intelligence chief, in turn, became the stuff of legend. There are few parallels in history (in a democratic context) where the political and intelligence leadership have functioned in this manner, all the while strictly adhering to the norms of democratic conduct. It is to the eternal credit of DIB Mullick that he never ever breached the 'Lakshman Rekha' of professional conduct, a dictum that future heads of the Intelligence Bureau have tried to adhere to in their years in office.

I first met B.N. Mullick during 1955-56, as an IPS probationer. Mr. Mullick had come to deliver a talk at the Central Police Training College (since renamed as the National Police Academy). Mr. Mullick was no orator, but he held us spellbound with the clarity of his talk regarding arcane aspects of intelligence, as also the nation's future. The impression he created made many of us want to join the Intelligence Bureau—an organization about which hardly anyone of us knew anything. We were in total awe of the person, who, we were told had the ear of the Prime Minister, and was often consulted by him on state matters of the greatest importance.

A few years later (in February 1959), I joined the Intelligence Bureau under the Ear Marking Scheme, and had my first meeting with him in his office in South Block. He was then at the peak of his career, among the top four or five bureaucrats in the country, assisting the Prime Minister to chart the course of a nation, which had weathered its initial storms but was now beginning to face a multitude of new problems, mainly the threat from Pakistan and the incipient danger from China. He had unquestionable authority across the entire security spectrum. No one dared challenge his understanding of security issues. The solutions he proffered were almost always acted upon. In subsequent years, when I worked in close proximity with Mr. Mullick, this image of a man, who was in control of every situation he dealt with, was reinforced repeatedly.

India had been able to foil many of Pakistan's attempts to destabilize India, through good intelligence, but intelligence on China was proving to be a more serious problem. India had warmly welcomed the advent of Communist China, but it was apparent to Indian Intelligence that China had certain ulterior designs of its own. DIB Mullick, thus found himself racing against time to build a strong intelligence network to counter China's designs. This included undertaking a multitude of intelligence tasks, such as the setting up of a chain of check posts on the Sino-Indian border.

The entire structure of intelligence gathering had also to undergo a massive change. New methods of intelligence collection and assessment were introduced. New personnel policies were contrived. Mr. Mullick came up with the concept of the Ear-Marking Scheme by which a few select young police officers were inducted into the IB each year, to form the nucleus of an intelligence cadre. The objective was increased professionalism in the higher ranks of the Intelligence Bureau. Alongside this, more modern tools of intelligence collection, analysis, and assessment were also introduced.

The 1960s were not a particularly propitious period for India and Indian intelligence. China seemed to become increasingly belligerent and to resent India's leadership of the non-aligned world. The Sino-Indian border also became more live. All these added to the problems of the Indian Intelligence Establishment and of Director Mullick.

Consequently, several more steps had to be initiated to enhance intelligence vigil, not only on the border but also to gauge China's true intentions. DIB Mullick was a proponent of the Forward Policy, which simultaneously putting in pace an effective early warning system, anticipating a possible Chinese attack on Indian positions along the entire border.

Unfortunately, before many of the steps could be effectively put in place, China launched an all-out attack on Indian positions in both Ladakh and Arunachal Pradesh. China's advance in both sectors, and India's partial retreat from both the regions, were construed as a setback to Indian Intelligence and the nation. It tended to diminish Director Mullick's image along with that of Prime Minister Nehru. This placed the Intelligence Bureau in a difficult situation.

The 1962 setback might have deterred a lesser man, but not Mr. Mullick. He used the setback to completely refurbish the Intelligence Bureau, and give a new shine to India's approach to the craft of intelligence. Between November 1962 and early 1964, he created a host of new institutions, providing a new impetus to technological aids to intelligence gathering. Likewise, new methods of intelligence assessment and intelligence analysis were introduced. In less than three years, during one of the darkest periods in the history of Indian intelligence, Mr. Mullick, thus, revolutionized the discipline of intelligence in India.

During this period, Mr. Mullick was responsible for the setting up of the highly sophisticated (and at the time super secret) body, which went by the name of Aviation Research Centre. It employed both aviation and modern technology to collect intelligence far beyond the borders of the country, and supplement the human intelligence available from deep penetration sources inside countries like China and Pakistan. He also established the Indo-Tibetan Border Force, to man and supplement the existing intelligence check-posts on the Indian-China border, both in Ladakh and Arunachal Pradesh. He created a Special Unit, whose nomenclature has undergone many changes over the years, viz. the SFF, to carry out daring operations across the border, mainly in Tibet. He also formed a stay-behind intelligence organization, designated as the Special Security of the Border Force (SSB) to act as a fifth column, if the enemy overran Indian territory. Each of these organizations continued to this day, but have since metamorphosed into separate organizations.

Prime Minister Nehru died in May 1964. Mr. Mullick, who by then had a series of extensions in service, chose to step down from office thereafter the same year. Thus, ended what may be termed as the Mullick era in modern India's intelligence history.

By then, Mr. Mullick had made a significant contribution to India's national security establishment, dominating not only the intelligence establishment, but the police as well. As the country's foremost policeman for nearly a decade and a half, he did more than any other policeman till that date to foster cooperation and coordination among the police forces of the country. He encouraged cross-pollination among the police forces of the country. He employed the annual meeting of Deputy Inspectors General CID of the different states in the country, as also the bi-annual meetings of the Inspectors General Police (he presided over both), to provide a unity of purpose and common national objective among the country's police forces. The importance he attached in this same context to achieving fellow-feeling among the country's police forces by sponsoring the All India Police Games and the All India Police Duty Meet also need to be recognized.

An important tradition he established was a close relationship with the head of the Central Bureau of Investigation, which had evolved in the 1960s from the Delhi Special Police Establishment into the Central Bureau of Investigation. The premier investigative agencies of the country acting in tandem, had a salutary impact on the nation's psyche. As more Central Police Organizations came into existence, this tradition set by the Intelligence Bureau and the Central Bureau of Investigation became the norm. The result has been a unified sense of direction regarding police functioning across the entire country, which include both the state and central police forces.

The Mullick chapter did not come to an end with his stepping down from the post of Director, Intelligence Bureau. Coinciding with the 1965 war with Pakistan, Mr. Mullick was persuaded to become the Director General of Security, to ensure the smooth functioning and better integration of the many new security and intelligence organizations that he himself had established in the wake of the 1962 conflict with China. Mr. Mullick finally stepped down only in 1966. For the remaining period of his life, and till his death in 1984, he became a near-ascetic, but was available when required for consultations.

Mr. Mullick was a man with a mission. His vision was to protect India from both internal and external enemies and his choice of weapons was intelligence and the security establishment. He was available to the country during the early formative years of post-independent India, during which period, he performed with both conspicuous skill as well as dedication.

Mr. Mullick had an encyclopaedic mind as far as security and intelligence subjects were concerned. He had a clear sense of what was right and what was wrong. He was honest, secular and above all a remarkable human being. It is difficult to say whether he saw himself as a man of destiny, but clearly destiny had marked him out for its own. Those of us, who were privileged to work with him, further believe that it was our great good fortune that we had an opportunity to do so.

2

V.G. Kanetkar: A Man of Honour

Julio Ribeiro

An apocryphal story was told about Vishnu Gopal Kanetkar that he ordered the prosecution of his own wife for contravening a traffic law! When I joined the Service in 1953, I heard this story, believed it and was in awe of the man ever since.

Many years later, when I was given my first charge of a district called Parbhani in Maharashtra, I received a phone call from none other than this great police leader. He wanted to know more about my batchmate and close friend, Dattatraya Shankar (Vasant to his family) Soman—the information, he told me in confidence, was required, because of a proposal his wife's family was about to make to my dear friend's parents. I was overawed at that time, but exulted later, when the match materialized.

In my opening paragraph I mentioned that the story of Mr. Kanetkar ordering the prosecution of his own wife for a traffic offence was "apocryphal". I used the adjective because later during my service years I heard a similar story "mutatis mutandis", about M.G. Pimaputkar, an ICS officer who was the Municipal Commissioner of Bombay (as the city was then called) when Kanetkar was the Police Commissioner. It became obvious to me that the awe that surrounded the ICS and IP officers of that era often resulted in such myths. But the imaginative minds that spun such stories did manage to convey a message to young entrants to the Services and that message was "Beware of even minor transgressions when interacting with officers whose moral timbre is well above the ordinary".

Vishnu Gopal Kanetkar was born on September 15, 1911 in a small village near the district town of Sholapur. His father, who died at a young age, was a Supervisor in a cotton mill in Sholapur (incidentally, one former IP officer, an Englishman named Dodwell, was the Manager of that mill when I served as Superintendent of Police, Sholapur, from 1962 to 1964).

Kanetkar's uncle, a medical doctor, brought up young Vishnu after his father's death. The old doctor was enamoured of Sanskrit. He taught Vishnu that ancient language but did not have the money needed to send his nephew to England to appear for the ICS examination.

Vishnu Kanetkar took the alternative route to covenanted service. He appeared for the IP selection after graduating from Pune's Fergusson College with honours. He was selected to join a small band of IP officers of Indian origin—some 8 or 9 at the time of his entry—and a larger number of Englishmen recruited in the United Kingdom. He was inducted into the IP cadre of the erstwhile Bombay Province, which included Sindh (now in Pakistan) and parts of Maharashtra, Karnataka and Gujarat.

Known to be a strict disciplinarian, he could be at the same time compassionate and understanding. He had a great sense of justice and embodied the concept of service as an essential part of his personality and philosophy of life.

I asked his son, Ashok, a cardio-vascular surgeon, about the legends surrounding his father. Instead, he spoke of his own childhood experiences of being disciplined by his father. A constable on guard duty at his father's residence allowed young Ashok to take a drag at the "bidi" the man was smoking. One drag was enough to result in a violent fit of coughing, which attracted the attention of his father who was working in his bungalow office. Ashok was administered a tight slap and the policeman sent back to the lines. No other punishment was given to the constable as Ashok's father felt it would be unfair and disproportionate to the offence.

Mr. Kanetkar was a staunch nationalist. He had joined the Mahatma in the famous Dandi March. Fortunately, the CID of the colonial times did not ferret this titbit of information and cleared this future doyen of great police leaders for entry into the IP. But as Ashok, his son, told me "his love and desire for an independent India did not in any way affect his role as a sincere and dedicated police officer in the British Raj."

Mr. Kanetkar was the Superintendent of Police of Poona (now Pune) when the Chief Minister Morarji Desai asked him if he was willing to go to Rajkot as IGP of the newly formed state of Saurashtra. A dacoit named Bhupat was spreading terror across the former territories ruled by sundry princes. It was common for a small prince to harbour or even employ dacoits who then led sorties into adjoining states and returned with booty that was shared by impecunious Rajkumars.

Bhupat and his gang was responsible for several murders and dacoities across Saurashtra. Kanetkar learnt that Prince Nirmal Kumar of Navanagar was Bhupat's benefactor. He summoned the prince to his office in Rajkot and confronted him with the evidence he had gathered to prove the prince's patronage and complicity in crimes. The prince had to accept his guilt—he was arrested after Prime Minister Nehru was informed. Bhupat escaped to Pakistan, never to return. His main henchman Devayat was tracked down and shot. Bachu, the last of the absconding gangsters was soon arrested. And thus was the scourge of the notorious dacoit Bhupat eliminated by the painstaking efforts over a period of time by Vishnu Gopal Kanetkar.

After succeeding in Saurashtra, Mr. Kanetkar was shifted to the neighbouring state of Rajasthan which was formed after the amalgamation of several princely states, some of them like Jaipur and Jodhpur. He was expecting to be rewarded with the highest post any police officer could attain in those days, the director of the Intelligence Bureau, but that was not to be.

However, he was made the Commissioner of Police, Bombay, in January 1960, a post he held with aplomb till March 1962. He was known for his rigid adherence to all rules and regulations, to all norms of etiquette and good conduct, to truth, justice and dedicated service to the people he served. While looking after the welfare and working conditions of his officers and men and treating them sympathetically, he also made it clear that corruption and misconduct had no place in his scheme of things. And the officers and men of Bombay City Police knew exactly where the lines were drawn.

Mr. Kanetkar had lost his faith in God when he learnt that the dacoit Bhupat visited Somnath regularly. He could not reconcile this religiosity with the fact that the believer had the blood of eighty human beings on his hands. But, his foray into atheism did not prevent him from reading a chapter from the Gita every day. His 'young' friend and daily walking companion, the ex-DIB V. G. Vaidya, has an interesting take on his senior's atheism. Kanetkar did not believe in the existence of God, but, says Vaidya only God could have created a person as rare as Mr. Kanetkar.

Vaidya compiled a booklet with ten essays authored by Mr. Kanetkar himself after his retirement. The booklet titled *The Rare Policeman* was published by the "Centre for Police Research", Pune, on September 15, 2011. It gives the reader an insight into the personality of this great police leader who was never afraid to express his views even if they attracted criticism or even worse, enmity. His letter to Prime Minister Vajpayee with his radical views on the Kashmir imbroglio will not endear him to most of his countrymen. But he voiced his views nonetheless because he thought that truth lay in many of the assertions he had made in his letter.

Vishnu Gopal Kanetkar was the first Director of the CRPF and a much admired Commissioner of the Bombay (now Mumbai) Police. His name is forever etched in the annals of the Maharashtra Police and the Indian Police as a man of integrity, whom no force on earth could dislodge from the path of duty and honour.

3

K.F. Rustamji: The Man Who Saw Tomorrow

S.K. Sharma

K.F. Rustamji is perhaps the most written about police officer in post independent India because of his very charismatic personality, far-reaching vision and total commitment which he brought to bear on the responsibilities and missions he was entrusted with during his long police career in the state of Madhya Pradesh, and equally in the central government. Going through the numerous writings and my own ringside view and his I found that Mr. Rustamji's perception of his responsibilities extended way beyond what the normal scope of that role would appear to the general rung of officers. There are any number of examples in the various writings on Mr. Rustamji to illustrate this aspect and a few of these are quoted in this article too, which show how his superior vision and courage of conviction enhanced the quality of services rendered by the organizations he served and how he raised their image and status.

If the quality of a leader is known by the standards he set for himself, then Rustamji began climbing the steps to glory early in his life by scoring many firsts and other impressive milestones. Digging into his past one finds that he topped the Nagpur University in the MSc in 1936; topped the All-India competitive examination for selection in the Indian Police (IP) in 1938; was awarded the Indian Police Medal in a record span of 4 years of service for exemplary handling of a life threatening situation during serious riots in Nagpur; became the country's youngest Inspector General of Police of a state (Madhya Pradesh) in 1958. He became the first police officer in the country to be bestowed with the rank of Director General superseding 25 officers and assigned the task of raising the Border Security Force under his command and control.

One of his high profile postings was the Chief Security Officer of the first Prime Minister of India, Pandit Jawaharlal Nehru, for nearly 7 long years, when he was on deputation with the Central Intelligence Bureau. Pt. Nehru was a man of the masses and a household name along with Mahatma Gandhi as the leading lights of the India Independence Movement. Massive crowds thronged to see him when he toured the length and breadth of the country. The assassination of Mahatma Gandhi in 1948 had tremendously increased the security threat to Pt. Nehru. He loved to be with the masses and would not brook any attempt to keep them away from him on grounds of security. Sometimes, he lost his temper with the police on duty on this account. The officialdom which accorded Nehru top priority to his security and safety, dared not tell him to adhere to the security procedures, due to his towering personality and family aura as also firm belief of being close to the people.

The security measures, therefore, had to be extremely unobtrusive as anything else would not find favour with the PM. This made the job of the Chief Security Officer all the more challenging and Rustamji chose to become virtually the PM's bodyguard to provide him proximate protection. He would usually even dress like Pt. Nehru and his close party followers, so as to not to be distinguishable as a policeman. And yet it is amazing that despite such a harrowing job, demanding the best physical and mental capabilities to handle unforeseen situations, Rustamji found time to regularly write notes on his observations and comments on the happenings of the day. The depth and quality of the content of these notes covering 1600 pages is evident from a beautifully curated book from these diaries titled *I Was Nehru's Shadow* edited by P.V. Rajgopal, IPS of the Madhya Pradesh cadre.

When Rustamji took over the reins of the Madhya Pradesh Police in 1958, the dacoity menace in the state was at its peak. His innovative strategies in engaging with notorious and dreaded dacoits led to an unprecedented number of successful police encounters culminating in the arrest or elimination of many dacoits including some notorious and dreaded giants like Gabbar Singh (relived in the popular film *Sholay*) who had become household names of those times. The police too suffered casualties including loss of life but the menace of dacoity in Chambal valley ravines had for once been tamed and the police had gained an upper hand over the dacoits in three years time. The heavy toll of life and the increasing police pressure through anti-dacoity operations and prosecutions of the captured dacoits forced the surviving dacoit leaders and their gangs to run for cover.

It was a matter of historical coincidence that in May 1960 when the Chambal dacoits were on the run, the venerable Acharya Vinoba Bhave decided to visit the Chambal ravines to spread a message of non-violence and peace to wean away the dacoits from their lives of crime and bloodshed. Acharya had information that the dacoits in hiding were tired of violence and depredations and they were keen to turn a new page in their lives. They were prepared to surrender along with their arms to Vinoba Bhave provided there were no police encounters or judicial executions and that their families were not harassed and their children's education was looked after by the state while they underwent imprisonment. Acharya Vinoba Bhave's peace march actually commenced in Chambal Ghati four days after a very daring and successful police operation in which a handful of police personnel had, at the risk of their lives, confronted a much larger gang of dacoits led by the dreaded Lakhan Singh and killed his right hand man in a boldly fought encounter against heavy odds.

Acharya Vinoba Bhave's peace march took him to the districts of Morena, Bhind Gwalior and Shivpuri, the main theatre of the dacoity menace. Acharya's peace mission had the patronage of the then Union Home Minister, Pt. Govind Vallabh Pant, as also of the state chief ministers of Madhya Pradesh and UP. The official history of the MP police records that 19 dacoits from these districts surrendered before Acharya over a period of three weeks of the peace march. However, the surrender of dacoits created new problems as the official agencies, especially, the police were not prepared for the implications and consequences of such a move. Nor was there any legal framework prepared by or for the peace mission laying down the terms of surrender. K.F. Rustamji, the then State Inspector General of Police who was responsible for the law and order in the state expressed the problem in the following words in a statement on June 2, 1961 which, I vaguely remember, had also appeared in the national media.

"It is a matter of regret that the mission should have deliberately given a setback to the task of maintaining law and order in the area in order to please the dacoits. Apart from operational time lost, and statements made against the police, the mission has delivered a blow to the morale of the force, because it has insulted the courage and devotion to duty of the men who stood up to fight the dacoits. At the time, the situation went out of control three years ago, when dacoit gangs roamed over the districts and killed, destroyed and raped in a manner unknown before, no outside help came to save us. It was policemen and the village lads and the best civil and police officers and men of the entire state who bore the brunt of the fury. It took three years for the police and people of these districts to turn the battle in their favour and when we are nearing the end, we are told that the courage and sacrifice of all was in vain, that the police officers who had shed their blood for defending others, had used a rifle and had thereby created dacoits, and that the dacoits sincerely feel that they have been oppressed by the police. The mission did not realize that if the area had not been controlled in time, a small pocket of hostile territory (Dakuland) would have been formed, cutting across the communications of India."

It appears that the media in 1961 was not any the less active and inquisitive than it is today. The Acharya was confronted with Rustamji's bold statement the very next day for his comments. Acharya's reaction to the statement sadly did not throw much light in defence of the missionary approach to the dacoity problem. As per the recordings of the police history, the Acharya said that only the person who made the statement knew about the problems as these problems were not before him (Acharya). He also added, "One sees God according to one's own light." When specifically asked to comment on the legal difficulties about the surrendered dacoits roaming free and yet wanted by the police and courts for heinous crimes as pointed out by IG Police, Acharya's reply was that he was not conversant with any law except the law of the Almighty. He quoted an English proverb saying "commonsense is nine-tenths of the law".

The then Chief Minister of MP, a stalwart politician, K.N. Katju, having been supportive of Acharya Vinoba Bhave's peace mission but also mindful of his position as CM of the state, however, reacted to the IGP's statement very responsibly, and while upholding the law of the land, fully supported his IGP. He said, "It is desirable that the offenders should not be glorified. They should be made to realize that they have committed serious crimes. It is not good that the dacoits should live in Acharya Vinoba Bhave's camp for days before being handed over to the authorities. It is desirable that if they surrender, they should be handed over for judicial custody, without any delay. I have seen some photographs in newspapers showing dacoits, who had surrendered, with garlands being feted. This is an utterly wrong thing."

The purpose of quoting the statements of Rustamji, Vinoba Bhave and K.N. Katju from the official history of the MP police is to illustrate how an IP officer heading the state police, had the courage of conviction and guts to freely express and forcefully confront the powers that be with his viewpoint of a dichotomous situation for the police force. And how a political head of the state government was bold enough to uphold the law even at the risk of causing serious embarrassment to his political seniors at the Centre. It is also noteworthy that Rustamji was in no way unmindful of the significance of a voluntary and non-governmental peace movement such as that of Acharya Vinoba Bhave to solve socio-criminal problems and issues. His concluding remarks are highly meaningful and showed a way forward which are equally relevant in today's scenario:

> I submit that if such a mission is sent again to deal with crime in an area, there should be special legislation which would enable it to act, and would remove the confusion and doubt in the minds of those who are charged with the duty of law enforcement. What is an official to do if the law of the land is contrary to the actions of the mission? What is a senior officer to do when he is told on the one hand that the mission is heavily supported, and on the other finds that it wants to get things done which are not in conformity with the law? Clearly there is a conflict between what the law requires and what the mission wants, and it is wrong to ask policemen to do what the mission wants. (Statement dated June 2, 1961 quoted in *MP Police History*).

Around the time of the Indo-Pak war-1965, the Government of India decided on the formation of the Border Security Force (BSF) to take the responsibility of centrally guarding the Indo-Pak border in place of the state police forces guarding the border in their respective states. The head of the proposed force was to be designated as Director General, higher in rank and pay than the State Inspectors General. In a meeting of state home ministers and IGPs called by the Centre to discuss this issue, Rustamji, the then IG MP Police was the lone voice to oppose the formation of a central force for border security in the central government. Ironically, it was he who was finally chosen to raise and head this force in the Home Ministry as its Founder Director General in 1965. Eventually, of course, all the chiefs of central and state police forces were raised to the level of Directors General. The following note found in Rustamji's diaries showcases the ease of mind, vision showing even some humour when he began to apply himself to the Herculean task of raising the Border Security Force:

> After handing over charge as IGP Madhya Pradesh, I reached Delhi and wrote my joining report on July 21, 1965... I became the head of a one man organization. I was the sole Borderman; nobody below me, nobody above me... After the Indo-Pak war, I went about the task of collecting men who would assist me in raising the force. I handpicked each one of them and got the best men from the police, the army, air force, the navy and the academic world. Many of the battalions belonging to the states manning the international border with Pakistan were taken over by us. Twenty-five battalions formed the BSF initially. Gradually we built up the strength by sending teams of officers to rural areas all over India to select the sturdy types and raised another twelve battalions. Fifteen more battalions deployed in Jammu and Kashmir were taken over in 1966 and within a year we had fifty-two battalions. The battalions belonging to the different states had their own strength and composition. It was necessary to bring about uniformity in the strength and composition by readjusting them. The process of reorganizing and readjusting increased the number of battalions to sixty.

The criteria of "handpicking' of officers to assist him in raising the Force and developing institutions and operational protocols was also set by Rustamji in very clear terms as:

> ...courage that is not affected by rumours or setbacks, strength of mind to judge and not be stricken by panic at any important moment, health, mental ability and educational background and finally, the ability to be a leader of men.

Raising, equipping and training the manpower to keep watch over an international border of 7,420 kilometres (including the erstwhile East Pakistan), with an inimical country in the neighbourhood, passing through a terrain ranging from deserts to coastal areas and mountains to plains cultivated to the last inch on both sides of the border was undoubtedly a gigantic task. The BSF was also to be responsible for "instilling in the panic-prone border population a sense of confidence in general" as per the Secretaries' Committee Report on the subject. The daunting challenge lay not in merely guarding the borders but to fashion a road map for development of various components of the Border Management in a holistic manner. It involved developing new concepts of training and skills for defensive and offensive roles usually in hostile terrains, survival kits and systems on snowy peaks, appropriate weaponry, setting up secured telecommunication channels and protocols, adequate peace and wartime medical cover in varying terrains and climes for BSF personnel and local populace, protocols for coordination with the Defence Services and central and state government agencies and hordes of associated supporting procedures and structures.

Rustamji went about tackling these humongous tasks with a high level of confidence and enthusiasm. The common strain that ran through the whole team was adoption of Innovation, Improvisation and Technology (IIT) to overcome the usual hurdles and bottlenecks in building up a new organization. He had developed an effective system of keeping a hawk's eye on all ongoing projects through the length and breadth of the Force to monitor the progress. This greatly inspired his large team of stalwarts and illustrious officers as also the men who felt the positive impact of his policies and planning whether they were on duty at their posts or off duty in the barracks. He was too impatient a man to take the beaten track and was simply not content with efforts made till the job was completely done. A sample of instances of adoption of the IIT approach and Rustamji's impatience with delays are illustrated below:

1. Soon after finding his feet as DG BSF he initiated a few basic actions well in advance, as these by nature were time consuming. One such action was placing a demand for bulk supply of cloth for uniforms on the Directorate. General of Supplies and Disposal (DG S&D) knowing supplies to government departments were beset with horrendous delays. When the supply was not made on time, Rustamji deputed an IG BSF to personally meet the Director General to expedite the supplies. The IG found that the textile mill was delaying the supply and that the functionaries in the office of the DG S&D were quite nonchalant about it. The IG knew that it would not be enough merely to report back on how matters stood. He, therefore, visited the textile mill himself. There he found out that the delay was in issuing of an import license for a particular dye by DG Foreign Trade. He then persuaded the DG FT and got them to provide the license to the textile mill and finally was able to get the supplies expedited from the textile mill to the BSF. That was a job completed in Rustamji's view.

2. Rustamji decided to computerize the payroll of the Force to ensure timely pay distribution among men posted all over the border areas. Computerization was hardly known in India in the 1960s. One of the first few essentials was to buy 4 imported machines to commence the technical side of the work. The minimum time for importing these machines was 4 months. Also government approval would be required. When I took the proposal for the import of these machines to Rustamji he first frowned upon the long delivery time. However when explained that the time period had been brought down from 8 to 4 months and the heavy machines would have to be surface transported from the UK and US, he relented. Then he complained that the government would take another six months at least to sanction the machines as they were not even conversant with the computers. He twirled his lips and said firmly, "Place the order directly on the firms. We don't have all that time for government approval" and returned the file to me unsigned. But before I could leave his room he again asked for the file and recorded the same words on the file and signed it. Then he looked at me, smiled and said, "I don't want them to catch you. Let them catch me. I know how to deal with them." Just as a corollary, I may add that I served the BSF for about six years thereafter and can authoritatively say that no notice was taken by the Home Ministry or any internal or external audit of this heavy, and unscheduled, expenditure which was not sanctioned through normal procedures. Thus he proved what he very often used to say in a lighter vein that "You can break every government rule provided you know how to do it."

While the size of the Force had grown to be over 100 battalions in about three years, it was the procurement of appropriate weaponry and communication equipment which faced insurmountable problems due to the acute shortage of foreign exchange in the country in the 1960s and 70s. Rustamji again showed the way by opening new frontiers of innovation and improvisation by recruiting more technical people and upgrading its existing workshops and opening new ones. The BSF history records the results of this enthusiasm of a young Force in being self-reliant in these words:

> ...the efficient technicians of the BSF got down to improvising the technology at their disposal and revolutionized radio communications in its workshops with marvellous ingenuity...The degree of self-sufficiency achieved by the young service like the BSF in the 1960s and 1970s was remarkable. Special workshops and factories were set up to overcome the shortage of arms and even produce fully functional 82mm mortars...

Encouraged by their success in technology conversion, the 'BSF technicians' ventured into their own rocket programme experimenting with short range missiles. Rustamji then enlisted the help of giant scientists like Vikram Sarabhai and A.P.J. Abdul Kalam who helped BSF make their own rockets with 20 Km reach in 1970 with effective results. "These rockets were used by the BSF for the first time in the Bangladesh conflict", said Rustamji, while recounting development of technologies in the BSF.

Sustained and carefully crafted capabilities built into a 6 years young Force was put to an acid test with the outbreak of tensions on India's borders with East Pakistan in 1971. The resultant Indo-Pak war, which broke out in December 1971, had actually started in March 1971 for the BSF to handle on its own. 25th March is a very significant day in the Indo-Pakistan history, when the people of East Pakistan openly rebelled against the long Pakistan rule of military tyranny on the East Pakistanis, leading to mass scale killings of innocent and some rebellious citizens and organized raping and killing of women and children by the Pak Army. Internal strife in East Pakistan seriously impacted the security of India, especially in the bordering areas. The BSF was fully alert and alive to these developments and did not take time in effectively securing its own side of the border even by crossing the international border to keep the hostile elements at bay. Their prompt and retaliatory actions encouraged the then East Pakistani liberation leaders and supporting private combatant groups to officially seek help from the Indian authorities. The Government of India, after due consideration of the pros and cons gave this delicate and sensitive role to Rustamji in the interest of security and sovereignty of India as also for protection of the human rights of the people of East Pakistan. The BSF history records that Indian operations in East

Pakistan had the approval of no less than the Prime Minister Indira Gandhi who told Rustamji, "Do what you like, but don't get caught." The BSF was fully empowered and made responsible to secure our national interests in all respects.

From March 25, to December 3, 1971, BSF's continuous operations won the Government of India and Indian Army's acclaim for the perfect covert and overt operations as well as actually fighting the hostile elements and the regular Pakistani troops. Finally, the Indian Army took over the direct command in December 1971 and their meticulous planning and heroic military action put the Pakistani troops on the run. With one stroke of his pen, Lt. Gen. J.S. Aurora, the Army Commander, took all of 90,000 troops of the Pakistan Army in East Pakistan into custody as PsOW and brought the 9 months saga of the Bangladesh Liberation Movement to a gloriously successful culmination for India and Bangladesh. The BSF's first taste of the war and its battle inoculation won the highest accolades from the then President of India V.V. Giri, the then Prime Minister Indira Gandhi and K.B. Lall, ICS the then Defence Secretary. To quote from the BSF History:

Prime Minister of India

Dear Shri Rustamji,

As the first line of our defence, the Border Security Force had to bear the immediate brunt of the enemy onslaught. The manner in which they faced enemy fire and the support they gave to the Army has played a crucial role in our ultimate success.

Our thoughts and prayers are with the families of the men and the officers who have sacrificed their lives in defence of India and her values.

I should like to express the gratitude of the government and the people of India to you and to your officers and men.

With kindest regards,

Yours Sincerely,
Sd/
(Indira Gandhi)

I feel the letter of K.B. Lall, the then Defence Secretary to the Government of India addressed to the Home Secretary on the successful culmination of the Indo-Pak War 1971 most aptly puts the role of Rustamji and BSF in the total war effort:

> ...A special word of thanks to the Director General of the Border Security Force and to the men and officers under his command is overdue. It is their initial initiatives, their boldness, courage and, if I may say so, imagination, which provided eventually an opportunity to the Defence Services to do their part. (*The Pioneer* of May 23, 2016 on Rustamji in the year of his birth centenary).

I would like to conclude this article with the words of Robin S. Sharma, a Canadian attorney of Indian origin, which to my mind very aptly describes the whole persona of K.F. Rustamji and his mission in life: "Leadership is not about a title or a designation. It's about impact, influence and inspiration. Impact involves getting results, influence is about spreading the passion you have for your work, and you have to inspire team-mates and customers."

P.S. Not many know about this but, in 1978, Rustamji visited the jails in Bihar and wrote about the conditions of the undertrials languishing for long periods. Two of his articles in *The Indian Express* formed the basis for the first Public Interest Litigation case—*Hussainara Khatoon vs State of Bihar*, which led to the release of 40,000 undertrials all over India.

4
Achievements of K.F. Rustamji

P.V. Rajgopal

After I obtained the permission of Khusro Faramurz Rustamji to write his biography, and before I could go through more than 10,000 pages of his handwritten diaries and typed articles, I interviewed him in his flat in Bombay. The first question I asked him was, "Sir, what do you consider as the three main achievements in your life?"

Without a moment's hesitation, his spontaneous reply was:

"Number 1—The PIL.
Number 2—My role in the Quit India Movement of 1942.
Number 3—Raising the BSF and nurturing it for nine long years."

He went on to elaborate these points. On the first point, he said that in December 1978, as a Member of the National Police Commission (NPC), he visited Karnataka, Maharashtra and finally Bihar. While the other members of the NPC were busy with police work, Rustamji visited the jails in these states. He was appalled by the conditions prevailing in the prisons. In Bihar, he went to the jails in Patna and Muzaffarpur. One by one, he called out the undertrials, who were in the prisons for the longest period and found out the details. He was astonished to see the magnitude and barbarity of the conditions prevalent in these two prisons and this made him seethe with indignation at what man could do to man, woman and child. Those poor, illiterate undertrials were caught in a cruel system, not knowing what to do and how to get out of the clutches of the law. He said, he "dipped his pen in venom"and sketched out the stories of some of the worst cases to show how oppressive and defenceless our criminal justice system had become for the poor, and how much blame lay with policemen, administrators, judicial officers and politicians, who tolerated such cruelties.

He submitted his write-up to *The Indian Express* newspaper, which published it as two separate articles on the front page on the January 8 and 9, 1979. The day, the second article appeared, he got a call from a lawyer, Kapila Hingorani, who stated that she and other lawyers discussed this with the Chief Justice of India, Justice Y.V. Chandrachud, and he was prepared to take up the case if he (Rustamji) was willing to give an affidavit regarding the facts published. Rustamji signed the two articles and a three-judge bench, headed by Justice P.N. Bhagwati, took it up as a Public Interest Litigation (PIL) for the first time in the judicial history of the country. The Supreme Court passed comprehensive orders and in consequence 40,000 undertrials, languishing in jails all over India for long periods, were set free.

This first PIL, based on his writings, raised a new hope in litigation. A person now has another forum which he can approach for redressal of his grievance against the government. It would come as a surprise to many, especially the anti-police types, that this new forum of redressal of civil liberties has come into existence owing to the efforts of a policeman—of all people.

In later life, Rustamji regretted that the surfeit of cases under the PIL has given rise to a new phenomenon of judicial activism, which has given rise to a feeling that the judiciary is extending its wings over matters, which are purely functions of the executive or the legislature.

On his second main achievement, Rustamji stated that in August 1942, he was posted as an Assistant Superintendent of Police (ASP) in Narsingpur in the then Central Provinces. He took leave and along with his childhood friend, Jal Cursetji (later Admiral of the Indian Navy) decided to go on a holiday to Kashmir. They halted for a few days in Nagpur, Rustamji's hometown, when riots due to the Quit India Movement broke out. Suddenly, one morning, a mounted constable came to his house with a note saying that he should report immediately to the Superintendent of Police of Nagpur, E.L. Treganza. Since the situation in Nagpur had taken a turn for the worse, Rustamji was recalled from leave and put on duty in the city. Two Army platoons and a magistrate, Michael Sullivan ICS, were attached with him.

At night a report was received that some 150 rioters were looting the food grain godown. He rushed in with a constable. Later, some more policemen arrived and there was a complete melee in the darkness with the looters trying to get out and the police attempting to rush in. Shortly afterwards, the Army platoons arrived and the Platoon Commander Lt Curtis started firing with his TMC. Three bullets whizzed past Rustamji, who screamed at Curtis to stop firing.

The following day, when they were going to the Police Lines, they were stoned heavily. Sullivan took a rifle from a policeman and started firing indiscriminately. Rustamji snatched the rifle from Sullivan. Another English military man fired from his revolver and killed a woman just because she threw a stone at him.

The next day, when he was at the boathouse on the tank, a convoy consisting of A.G. Scott, the IGP, G.W. Benton DIG and T.M. Collins DIG came there. Rustamji complained against Sullivan and the Army officers. As a junior ASP with just four years' service, and that too as an Indian officer, it required considerable temerity on his part to tell the three senior-most British masters that their method of dealing with the riots was wrong. He added that the normal Indian mob cannot maintain its frenzy for more than a week. Rustamji pleaded for time and patience and stated that unlimited use of force and indiscriminate suppression should not be resorted to. He said he was in favour of the use of minimum force. He concluded by saying that the economic compulsions of the poor people are such that no breakdown of law and order can continue for long. The British officers did not agree with him. They talked about the advancing Japanese army and believed that only indiscriminate use of force would suppress the 'rebellion', as they called it. They felt Rustamji was being too lenient and was told bluntly that he would be replaced from the charge of Nagpur city by another officer who would "batter the bastards" into submission. (By bastards they meant the Congress*walas*—their sworn enemies.)

Due to the stern action taken in the city, the agitation spread to the interior villages like Umrer, Khapa, the temple town of Ramtek and Moudha, where a revolutionary organization called the Hindustan Lal Sena, had declared independence from British rule for three days. Rustamji was sent to these places with a bare minimum force of 10 or 11 recruit constables. He faced grave danger to his life at these places but was able to establish law and order there.

When the disturbances subsided, Rustamji was posted to Ellichpur, a sub-division in Amravati district. Three months later, in November 1942, when he was still an ASP, he received a congratulatory telegram from the Governor of the Central Provinces stating that he had been awarded the Indian Police Medal by His Excellency the Viceroy of India. In February 1943, when he went to Nagpur to receive the Medal, he called on the IGP, Scott, who congratulated him and said, "Rustamji, we made a thorough appraisal of the situation after the disturbances and have come to the conclusion that your tactics were appropriate. The city was saved from much damage by the restraint that you urged on us. You were right. We were wrong. Hence the Medal."

Rustamji commented that it is only a Britisher, who could have said such a thing.

Regarding the third main achievement, Rustamji was hesitant

talking about his role in raising the Border Security Force. I had to prod him to talk about it, but did not succeed much. His diaries state that a high level meeting of the Home Ministers and Chiefs of Police of all the states was held in May 1965 to discuss the formation of a Central Force to guard the Indo-Pak border. At this meeting, presided over by Prime Minister Lal Bahadur Shastri, the only person who opposed raising the new Border Force was Rustamji himself. He did so, on grounds of economy. A few weeks later, he was summoned to Delhi and the Home Secretary, L.P. Singh took him to the Home Minister, Gulzarilal Nanda, who told Rustamji that he had been chosen to raise the new Border Force, with the elevated rank of Director General (DG) and an increase of Rs. 250 in his pay. Rustamji protested. He asked why he was being disturbed from his present position and why he was being chosen to head the new organization when there were so many officers senior to him. The Home Minister remarked all these factors were taken into consideration. In July 1965, Rustamji took over as DG of a non-existent force. For a few months, it remained a one-man force with nobody below him and no one above him.

During the course of my research, Golak Majumdar, who was at one time IG BSF of the Eastern Frontier, Calcutta, told me that he had once asked L.P. Singh ICS, who was Union Home Secretary for 13 long years, how the choice of the founder DG BSF fell on Rustamji, who was then comparatively junior, L.P. Singh told him that raising a new force was a Herculean task and he wanted someone, who had fire in his belly to be the first DG. He found Rustamji had that fire and he was made DG over the heads of 25 IP (Indian Police) officers senior to him. Most of the senior officers held responsible positions and they did not mind Rustamji taking over as the head of a non-existent Force in an elevated rank. However, there were many covetous eyes in the Army, but the Army Chief Gen J.N. Chaudhuri felt that the police force should be headed by a policeman and not a Lt Gen of the Army. L.P. Singh, who was then in retirement, remarked that it was one decision of his, he never regretted in his life.

Rustamji was used to writing a diary. It was always on a foolscap size paper. He started this habit on the day he was sent to a village Police Station for training as a Station House Officer in November 1938. He continued this practice right through his life—till the day he died in March 2003. In the diaries of 1965, he mentioned, in detail, the problems he had to face single-handedly in the initial days of raising the BSF. On September 1, 1965, the war with Pakistan had started. He was asked to go to Kashmir, where he had first-hand experience of war. His diaries of that period have interesting details of actual fighting on a day-to-day basis.

After the war, he handpicked officers from the Police, Army, Air Force, Navy and the academic world, who would assist him in raising the new Force. Thus, the BSF formally came into existence on December 1, 1965. Many of the state battalions manning the Indo-Pak border were taken over by the BSF. These 25 battalions formed the core of the BSF initially. Fifteen more battalions deployed in Jammu and Kashmir were taken over in 1966. In order to bring about uniformity, a reorganization of the strength of the battalions from different states was done. This increased the number to 52 battalions. New battalions were raised and within a year, the strength increased to 60 battalions.

One of the things a force requires is the facility for training. During the period he was IG MP, Rustamji found there were several palaces and buildings belonging to the Rajas and Maharajas, many of which were empty. He approached the Rajmata of Gwalior, Vijay Raje Scindia and asked her if the BSF could acquire the abandoned Palace in Tekanpur. She agreed. In 1966, the BSF paid a paltry amount of rupees six lakhs and forty-one thousand for the Palace and the huge parcel of land all around. The main training centre of the BSF was established there.

Rustamji admitted that in raising the BSF, the conditions proved fortuitous. It came at a time when the country needed such an organization. The just concluded Indo-Pak War produced a patriotic zeal which helped it to grow fast. Every ministry and every officer, even at the lowest level, was eager to help it to develop and expand rapidly. The Finance Minister approved the first BSF Budget without even looking into it. The Comptroller and Auditor General (CAG) of India instantaneously sanctioned a separate Pay and Account Office for the BSF. Parliament passed the BSF Bill without much discussion. The need was felt for suitable officers to man the various battalions. In 1966, the government sanctioned the creation of 66 posts of Assistant Commandants and later in 1968, approval was obtained for taking in 300 Emergency Commissioned Officers who were released by the Army.

The BSF's finest hour came in 1971, when it played a stellar role in the liberation of Bangladesh. In March 1971, disturbances broke out in the then East Pakistan. Sheikh Mujibur Rehman was arrested, martial law imposed and a crackdown was ordered. Several thousands were massacred. The Bengali troops in the East Bengal Regiment (EBR) and East Pakistan Rifles (EPR) revolted and it became a war between West Pakistan Muslims and the East Pakistan Muslims.

In New Delhi, the Parliament, which was in session, passed a Resolution assuring support and sympathy of the people of India to the 75 million people of East Bengal. This cleared the decks for action. Prime Minister Indira Gandhi gave a laconic direction to Rustamji—"Do what you like, but don't get caught." Nothing more was spelt out. This direction of the PM gave the BSF the liberty to enter the scene in the surcharged atmosphere and its commandos carried out tasks in support of the freedom fighters.

Immediately after, Tajuddin Ahmad, who was designated by Mujibur Rehman as his successor, and Amirul Islam, Chief Whip of the Awami League Party surreptitiously crossed the border and were received by the IG BSF, Golak Majumdar, who took them to Calcutta. He informed Rustamji, who reached there the same night and met the two leaders from East Pakistan. It was decided to take them to Delhi to meet Prime Minister Indira Gandhi.

Tajuddin was keen to form a formal government-in-exile. Arrangements were made to get as many of the recently elected members of the National Assembly from inside East Pakistan. Tajuddin also wanted Rustamji to personally take charge of the formation of the new government. Rustamji, on his part, was keen on having the swearing-in ceremony taking place on the soil of Bangladesh under the full gaze of the world press and TV cameramen, despite the ruthless aerial strafing being carried out by the Pakistan Air Force. A triangular piece of Bangladesh land jutting into India in the village called Baidyanath Tala, code named Mujib Nagar, was chosen.

The swearing-in ceremony site was kept a secret. The BSF

officers took the leaders to the site before 4 o'clock in the morning on April 17, 1971, to avoid the Naxalites. Rustamji went around with the BSF officers, P.R. Rajgopal and Golak Majumdar to satisfy himself about the arrangements and soon after left the place leaving behind the other two. The PRO of BSF took the world press to the place at the last moment. The function began at 11 o'clock. The Mukti Bahini boys, in their ragged uniforms, gave the Guard of Honour. The newly made flag of Bangladesh was unfurled. The newly selected national anthem was sung by some good singers of Krishna Nagar, selected by the BSF boys. The swearing-in of the cabinet was carried out under the mango grove and a proclamation read out by the new Prime Minister. This was covered by the world press and TV cameras. The new Constitution of Bangladesh drafted by Col N.S. Bains, Chief Law Officer of the BSF and vetted by a barrister of Calcutta was shown to the leaders and after minor corrections, was adopted by the new government.

Rustamji felt Pakistan would receive a bigger blow if the Deputy High Commissioner (DHC) of Pakistan based in Calcutta defected in favour of Bangladesh. Golak Majumdar, who was entrusted with this task, arranged a meeting between Hussain Ali, the DHC and Tajuddin. On April 18, 1971, Rustamji, Majumdar, Rajgopal and Maj Gen Narinder Singh organized the operation. By sheer coincidence, there was a rainstorm at 10 am and the Pakistani flag pole fell. It was immediately replaced by the Bangladesh flag. The BSF boys, who were ready with the new sign board removed the Pakistan High Commissioner's board and hammered in the Bangladesh board. In no time, huge crowds collected and there was wild cheering. The DHC defection encouraged Bengali diplomats in other countries to change their allegiance and strengthen the liberation struggle.

Rustamji felt that had the BSF not linked up with the Bengali officers and men who revolted, the liberation of Bangladesh might not have come as fast as it did. Rustamji met Mujibur Rehman in Dacca after the latter's release. The first comment Mujib made was, "So, you are Mr. Rustamji about whom I have heard so much."

In one of his diaries, Rustamji mentioned, "I often pride myself on one thing and that is that whatever event occurs in India, somehow or the other gets me involved in it." When one goes through his life, it becomes clear that this is not an empty boast.

After his role in the Quit India movement, he was involved in the integration of princely states post-independence. He then got involved in the Hyderabad Police Action of 1948. In 1952, he was taken on deputation to the Intelligence Bureau (IB) and functioned as Chief Security Officer to Prime Minister Jawaharlal Nehru for six long years. As Deputy Director in the IB, after a series of meetings with DIB B.N. Mullick, he drafted in 1957, the *Blue Book* for security of the VVIPs and arrangements at public meetings addressed by them. The instructions contained in this book are followed even to this day. Rustamji had a hobby of collecting figures of crimes committed all over India. He started producing a booklet *Crimes in India* from 1953 onwards till he left the IB in the middle of 1958. The government found these figures useful. Some years later, it led to the formation of the National Crime Record Bureau. Further, writing was a passion with him. He started the process of collecting articles on police and it led to the publication of the *Indian Police Journal* in 1954 and he was the Editor of the Journal for some years. The CBI came into existence in 1963. Earlier to that, the IB was also looking after specialized crime. Rustamji was in charge of this desk and in 1957, the major case he took up was regarding the scam that took place consequent on the nationalization of Insurance companies to form the Life Insurance Corporation (LIC). As Chief of the MP Police, his contribution to the elimination of the major dacoit gangs is phenomenal. After retirement from service, he was made Special Secretary in the Home Ministry. In this capacity, he was instrumental in the setting up of the Indian Coast Guard. The Rustamji Committee set up by the Cabinet submitted its recommendation in July 1975. Based on this report, the interim Indian Coast Guard came into existence in February 1977.

In 1977, when the Janata Government was in power, along with R.D. Singh, Director CBI, Rustamji met Jayaprakash Narayan (JP) and stressed the need to form a National Police Commission. JP passed on the suggestion to the government and a Commission was set up and Rustamji was appointed a Member.

For the services rendered during the Indo-Pak War, Rustamji was awarded the Padma Bhushan in 1972. His services after retirement were recognized by the award of the Padma Vibhushan in 1991—the first policeman to get the award.

In conclusion, I would like to quote what Rustamji had written in one of his articles. When he appeared before the interview Board for selection to the IP in 1937-38, one of the members of the Board was his old Principal of the Science College, Nagpur, where he studied. The British Principal, Prof. Morris Owen spoke for Rustamji even while he was still in the Interview Hall. Prof. Owen told the other members of the Board, "He is one of my best students. He deserves to be in the IP. Select him. And mark my words, gentlemen, this young man is going to go very high."

Now, in hind sight, we can say how true this Nostradamus-like prediction of the Englishman turned out to be.

After retirement, Rustamji was greatly sought after for his vast reservoir of experience. As Special Secretary in the Ministry of Home Affairs, he had a big hand in the structuring of Central Police Organizations, like the Indo-Tibetan Border Police and Central Industrial Security Force. He was a member of the National Police Commission from 1978 to 1983. Insightful and illuminating reports of the Commission bear the stamp of his clear and uncluttered thinking on various police issues. He lived a full glorious life, and the members of police forces, all over the country, cherish his memory, with love and honour.

5

R.N. Kao: Intelligence Chief Who Modelled India's External Strategic Security

Kalyan K. Mitra

Early Life and Induction in Intelligence Bureau (IB)

Rameshwarnath Kao, also known as Ramji Kao among his friends and colleagues, was born in the city of Varanasi in Uttar

Pradesh on May 10, 1918 to a Kashmiri Pandit family which migrated from Srinagar district. He died on January 20, 2002 in New Delhi. Kao was brought up by his uncle Pandit Triloknath Kao. He had his early schooling in the city of Baroda in the Bombay Presidency as it was known then. After obtaining his Master of Arts degree in English literature from Allahabad University, he joined the Imperial Police (IP) in the year 1940. His first posting was as Assistant Superintendent of Police, Kanpur. He was deputed to the Intelligence Bureau (IB) which was being reorganized by B.N. Mullick on the eve of independence in 1947. Kao was given charge of VIP security and entrusted with the task of looking after the security ring around Prime Minister Jawaharlal Nehru. In the late 1950s, he was sent to Ghana to help the government of Prime Minister Kwame Nkrumah in setting up an intelligence and security organization in that country.

Tall, handsome, suave and intellectual in the true sense of the word, Rameshwarnath Kao remained a shy person till the last day of his life. A thoroughly well-mannered gentleman, he shunned publicity and preferred not to talk about his professional exploits which lesser mortals would have turned into volumes of printed words. Kao was rarely seen in public. As chief of India's first External Intelligence Agency, Research and Analysis Wing (R&AW), he maintained links and contacts in the intelligence community across the world. Count Alexandre de Marenches, Head of the French Service for External Documentation and Counter-Intelligence (SDECE) had this to say about Kao and I quote "what a fascinating mix of physical and mental elegance. What accomplishments! And yet so shy of talking about himself."

Kao and the "Kashmir Princess" Probe in 1955

The following episode has been recorded by B.N. Mullik in his book *My Years with Nehru: The Chinese Betrayal*. I narrate the story briefly in the following paragraphs:

Air India International super constellation plane (Lockheed L-749 A) "Kashmir Princess" was chartered by the Chinese delegation to attend the Afro-Asian Conference at Bandung (Indonesia). The plane was chartered to take Chinese Prime Minister Chou En-Lai, who changed his plan at the last minute and travelled via Kunming,

Rangoon and Singapore. The aircraft carried some junior Chinese officials and representatives from the Press. The aircraft caught fire after taking off from Hong Kong on April 11, 1955. People across the world were shocked by this incident which later turned out to be an act of sabotage by a Kuomintang (KMT) agent in order to assassinate Chou En-Lai. As the act had taken place in Hong Kong, local British authorities and the then British Prime Minister, Sir Anthony Eden, had given public assurance that the guilty would be brought to book. The Chinese government, however, insisted that Indian officials should be associated with the enquiry. Before his departure for Bandung, Nehru told B.N. Mullik that a senior Indian officer should be sent to Hong Kong to be associated with the enquiry. B.N. Mullick selected R.N. Kao, Assistant Director in charge of security, for this purpose.

Kao arrived at Jakarta on April 23, 1955, where he met Pandit Nehru and Chinese Prime Minister Chou En-Lai, who invited him to come to Peking where all the material obtained by the Chinese government would be handed over to him. Kao went to Peking on 7th May and had several meetings with Chou En-Lai. He returned to Hong Kong on 18th May, accompanied by Deputy Director, Information, Ministry of Foreign Affairs, People's Republic of China (PRC) and began to interact with both the British authorities and the Chinese officer. He kept the IB Headquarters and Mullick in the picture about the progress of investigation from time to time.

Kao did all that could be done and finally returned on 15th September. He went to Peking twice and held several meetings with Chou En-Lai, who was cordial and polite to him although at one stage, Chou had made unfounded allegations regarding the progress of enquiry. He tried to get an admission of sorts from Kao that the British authorities were not interested in investigating the case properly. Kao stood his ground and maintained that the British had done everything possible. As the accused person had escaped to Formosa, nothing more could be done. Chou En-Lai wanted Kao to sign a joint report with Chinese officials but Kao did not agree to do so. Eventually, the British government closed the case in December. During the entire period of the investigation, Nehru supported and demonstrated his complete trust in Assistant Director Kao, wrote B.N. Mullick in his book.

Career Progression

Kao's professional skill was well regarded not only by Nehru but Indira Gandhi as well. He also served as Security Advisor to Rajiv Gandhi. His proximity to Indira Gandhi aroused suspicion in some quarters within the political class about his role during the infamous "Emergency". But unknown to many, Kao had privately cautioned Indira Gandhi and advised her not to declare the Emergency. When Morarji Desai came to power, he resigned and returned when Indira made a comeback in 1980.

In the days following the 1962 debacle, Kao played a stellar role in the Directorate General of Security which was set up in 1965. After retirement, B.N. Mullick was reappointed as the first DG Security by Prime Minister Lal Bahadur Shastri. Kao was posted as the first Chief of the super secret Aviation Research Centre (ARC) an organization under B.N. Mullick. ARC had the charter of collecting technical intelligence including Communication Intelligence (COMINT), Electronic Intelligence (ELINT), Signal Intelligence (SIGINT), Imagery Intelligence (IMINT), etc. Later, Kao himself founded India's first external intelligence agency, Research and Analysis Wing (R&AW) in September 1968. The rest is history.

Kao in the Eyes of an Eminent Civil Servant

Naresh Chandra, former Cabinet Secretary, India's Ambassador in USA and also ex-governor of Gujarat knew R.N. Kao very well. He delivered the Kao Memorial lecture in January 2012 at the R&AW Headquarters. Referring to Kao, as the creator of ARC and R&AW, Chandra made special mention of Kao's behind the scene contribution to India's military victory in the Indo-Pak War in 1971. He noted that the significant feature of Kao's vision for the R&AW was to lay strong emphasis on the quality of manpower and the multi-disciplinary sources from which select personnel should be drawn and motivated for the complex tasks entrusted to the organization. Chandra also referred to the fact that Kao had realized the importance of working with agencies of other countries to optimize the quality of analysis generated by different agencies. Naresh Chandra recalled his last meeting with "Kao Saheb" in March 2001 when he returned in Delhi from Washington DC. He said that Kao's analysis of India-US relations and knowledge of the current situation was impressive as always. Naresh Chandra observed that he would for ever cherish the way Kao Saheb could put junior officers at ease.He also said that Mr. Kao had a keen sense of humour, amazing human touch and true love for the arts.

My First Meeting with Mr. Kao and Subsequent Interaction

The year was early 1964. I was Assistant Superintendent of Police, Bhubaneswar, capital of Orissa state (now known as Odisha). I received a telephone call from IB's Central Intelligence Officer (CIO) posted at Cuttack. He told me that a very senior and important officer of the IB a certain Mr. Kao would be arriving by air from Delhi and I should go to the airport to receive him, take him to the state guest house and remain with him till CIO's arrival. I went to the airport in uniform. I saw several foreigners getting down from the aircraft. One of them was very handsome and the tallest was wearing a white shirt and corduroy trousers. On closer look, I realized that he was actually an Indian. I went forward, saluted him and introduced myself. After we reached the guest house, he asked me the usual questions about my academic background, hobbies and so on. I saw him off later at the railway station as he planned to go to Calcutta by train.

Our next meeting took place in February 1969. I received him at Charbatia, the main base of ARC. Mr. Kao was the Chief of R&AW at that time. When he settled down at the VVIP Room, he thanked me, took one look at me and said that he remembered me and our meeting in Bhubaneshwar five years ago. He also told me that my IG, R.K. Padhi was his good friend. At that point of time, I was Assistant Director in charge of Administration. R. Swaminathan, the other Assistant Director, was in charge of secret and sensitive intelligence operations. He was promoted and posted to headquarters as Joint Deputy Director and frequently visited Charbatia. Several months later, Swaminathan told me that Mr. Kao had decided to post me as Assistant Director (Intelligence) and had told my IG R.K. Padhi that he would like me to continue on deputation to ARC. As things turned out, I never went back to my parent cadre. As AD(I) Charbatia, my task was to supervise technical intelligence operations in order to watch Tibet and military developments in China in collaboration with friendly agencies. Eventually, I moved to headquarters, took charge of the Tibet desk and was understudy to the Deputy Director in charge of the China desk.

During the Indo-Pak War of 1971, Mr. Kao and his team played a crucial role by creating 'Mujib Nagar', training 'Mukti Vahini', arming and air dropping them at pre-designated zones inside the then East Pakistan. The operations prepared the ground for the final military victory under the command of General Manekshaw. During the operations, Kao was ably assisted by his esteemed colleague from IB P.N. Banerjee. I played my allotted role while posted at Charbatia for which I was duly awarded the 'Sangram Medal' and 'Poorvi Star'.

During my post retirement days, I used to meet Mr. Kao frequently at his residence. On one occasion, I asked Mr. Kao how, in his view, posterity would judge Indira Gandhi. He remained silent and thoughtful for a while and said, "Harshly, I believe, in spite of all that she did for the country, victory in the Indo-Pak War of 1971 and Liberation of Bangladesh." History has proved Mr. Kao right. Posterity seems to have remembered Indira Gandhi for the 'Emergency' days and not for her role during the 1971 war. It seems Shakespeare correctly made Mark Anthony say, "The evil that men do lives after them; the good is oft interred with the bones."

I used to plead to Mr. Kao that he might consider recording or keeping notes of those eventful days. He told me that such disclosures would only benefit our adversaries. But I learnt later that he had recorded his notes which have been kept in the Nehru Museum Library. He had reportedly given instruction that these notes should be made public long after he breathed his last.

Someone from the media asked me recently if I could throw some light on Mr. Kao's ideas and perceptions regarding China and the likely future scenario in Asia and the world in the wake of China's steady rise as an economic giant and military super power. I told him that Mr. Kao was truly far-sighted. His views and perceptions were almost prophetic and valid today. To prove my point, I reproduce below a letter ne sent me after reading one of my articles published in the *USI Journal* in 1996.

My dear Mitra, September 2, 1996

Thank you very much for sending to me through B.P.S. Kapoor, a copy of your article "China in the 21st Century—Implications for India," which was published in the April-June 1996 journal of the USI.

This is a very impressive piece, and may I offer you my felicitations on the profundity of your article? Its scope is as impressive as the compulsive logic of the data presented by you. I wholly agree with what you have stated in the conclusion. The only imponderable, which I see in China's future, flows from the fact that when people become economically prosperous they begin to think for themselves and this thought process can be quite explosive. One does not know how far the Chinese government would succeed in harmonizing economic affluence with political rigidity.

With thanks again and hoping that you both are in good health and keeping yourself usefully employed.

Warm regards from my wife and me to Mrs. Mitra and you.

Yours sincerely,
R.N. Kao

Mr. Kao had a special love for the arts. In fact, he was a fine sculptor himself. His Vasant Vihar home has quite a few splendid creations in marble, ceramic, fibre glass, plaster of Paris, bronze and wood. He had special fascination for horses and made one in fibre glass. I have often wondered how a person with the heavy burden of official work of national importance could also pursue his passion for artistic and creative work. Indeed, it is a truly mind blowing feat which only an exceptionally gifted and very hard working person can achieve. Ramji Kao was one such multi-talented person.

As I end this narrative which is a homage paid to the most wonderful leader of men and a great human being, I cannot help recalling that whenever my wife and I left Mr. and Mrs. Kao after a visit to his home, he would invariably come out to see us off. I always protested and he would always tell me that he came out to see off my wife and would also do so in future. May God grant him eternal peace.

6

Ranjit Kumar Gupta: His Life and Career

Ashok K. Abrol

When Socrates was explaining to his judges how it was that he had made himself so unpopular, he told them of his investigations into the wisdom of those whom the world reputed to be wise. While it is a matter of immense pride to be called upon to write about Ranjit Kumar Gupta, or simply Ranjit Gupta, as he was popularly known, I feel a slight trepidation lest I too should be hauled up before a jury. The exercise of evaluating the life and career of Ranjit Gupta who was head and shoulders above all of us in the cadre, and that too in this short space, can be quite a challenge because the real Ranjit Gupta remained so elusive. His was a flamboyant, multifaceted, and unfathomable persona that would not fit into a straitjacket. He was not only an archetypal police officer but also an astonishingly remarkable man, complete with warts and all. A hard taskmaster with strong likes and dislikes and a gourmet to the core, it is no wonder that some of my colleagues chose to describe him as "the last Mughal" among the bureaucrats of Bengal. I have been privy to situations where his word as the IGP carried more weight than that of the Home Secretary, if not that of the Chief Secretary. Siddhartha Shankar Ray, the Chief Minister of West Bengal (from 1972 to 1977), looked up to his IGP, though Ray was a good 6/7 inches taller.

If a genius is "one per cent inspiration, ninety-nine per cent perspiration", then Ranjit Gupta—the quintessential super cop and arguably, one of the most erudite and eminent in the country—was certainly a genius par excellence: He was doubtlessly ninety-nine per cent perspiration, but he was also gifted with ninety-nine per cent inspiration by his Maker. A maverick, he was possessed of the most brilliant talents and a vast range of interests. He excelled in every department and had immense reserves of energy—be it intellectual pursuits, sportsmanship or professional skills. We often used to wonder, as to how this man could fit so much into a day.

Ranjit Gupta's original discipline at Presidency College was History, which he had read under the legendary teacher Susobhan Sarkar. It is noteworthy that Ranjit Gupta was the only contributor to the Festschrift, brought out to honour his old master, who was not a practising academician, while all the other contributors happened to be big names from the discipline of History. From Applied Anthropology to Zoology, Ranjit Gupta could discuss any subject under the sun. Military History was of course his forte and his knowledge of weaponry could easily put an Army Brigadier to shame, but he was equally conversant with the writings of Marx, Lenin and Mao, not to mention Tagore, Milton and Shakespeare. During an 'interview' at Writers' Building in 1974, when I mentioned that I was from district Gurdaspur of Punjab, my IGP promptly asked me whether I had read Tagore's well known poem "Bandi Veer" about the exploits of Sardar Banda Singh Bahadur, who had been imprisoned in Gurdaspur Fort by the Mughals before he was blinded, maimed and killed in 1,716. Unfortunately, I drew a blank, but after coming out of Writers' Building, I immediately ran to Bow Bazaar and bought myself a copy of *Sanchaita*—a marvellous collection of Tagore's chosen poems, which continues to adorn my bookshelf till this day and is one of my favourite reference books.

Ranjit Gupta's scintillating witticisms are remembered till date by the old timers in the service who were always awe-struck and tongue-tied in his presence. His amazing equestrian skills, his love of horses and the dynamic game of polo have been a part of the urban folklore in police circles of West Bengal. He went on to become the President of the Calcutta Polo Club and was a delegate to the Indian Polo Association. A fitness freak, he religiously continued his 'work outs' well into his 70s and 80s. He survived cancer of the colon and lived with a pacemaker in his heart. He wielded his pen and "baton" with equal might and his professional commitments notwithstanding, Ranjit Gupta found time to contribute exceptionally well-written and reasoned articles for various newspapers and periodicals. Mention may be made of his award winning article in the Centenary issue of *The Statesman* in April 1975, titled "Time Does Not Have a Stop" and the exquisite essay titled "The Revolutions that Failed" in the now defunct *Illustrated Weekly of India* of April 21, 1985.

This colossus was born in Dacca (now Dhaka) into a Baidya family on February 9, 1920. Those familiar with the history of East Bengal would be able to appreciate the true import of this genealogy. He joined the Imperial Police during the twilight years of the Raj on March 3, 1942 and was trained along with Taslimuddin Ahmed, who went on to become the IGP of East Pakistan (now Bangladesh). Between 1943 and 1947 he served in various capacities, including SDPO in Chittagong District (pre-independence Bengal), where he was responsible for liaison with the Indian Army during the Second World War. When the war ended, he was posted as SDPO, Serampore where R.N. Sengupta (who later became the Chief Secretary), was the SDO.

After independence, Ranjit Gupta was posted to Calcutta as the Superintendent of Police (Wireless). The police communication system in West Bengal was in shambles. He supervised the installation of an upgraded wireless system for the state and for the city of Calcutta alike—a system that has stood both the police forces in good stead ever since. Ranjit Gupta's rise in the service was swift, at times spectacular. While this had much to do with his competence and dedication, the promotion process was also accelerated by the vacuum created by the movement of many senior police officers to "East Pakistan". In 1948 he became the Deputy Commissioner of Police (South) in Calcutta when he was just 28. He also served for a few months as Deputy Commissioner of Police, Detective Department. In 1951, he was posted as SP, Burdwan and in 1953, as SP, Midnapore. In 1955, he re-joined the Calcutta Police organization as Deputy Commissioner of Police (HQ), and played a seminal role in improving the training and discipline of the Force through a slew of bold and novel initiatives.

A number of anecdotes are popular among the old-timers in the West Bengal Police about Ranjit Gupta's tenure as DCP (HQ), his wry sense of humour, his unmistakable aura of authority and of course, 'eccentricities'. An apocryphal story about his indirect brush with Morarji Desai is particularly amusing. Morarji Desai, who was Chief Minister of Bombay State from 1952 to 1956, (before 'Bombay' was bifurcated and reorganized on a linguistic basis as Maharashtra and Gujarat) was moving to Delhi to take over as the Union Minister of Commerce & Industry in Jawaharlal Nehru's government. Being a devout Hindu, he wanted to visit his Guruji near Calcutta for his blessings before assuming charge as a Cabinet Minister, and had chosen to make this detour. An aide called up Ranjit Gupta in Lal Bazaar requesting for some security arrangements at Dumdum Airport and an escort for Mr. Morarji Desai. "Who is Morarji Desai?" asked Ranjit Gupta in his characteristic deadpan style. "Sir, he is the Ex-Chief Minister of Bombay state", said the aide as he wanted to remain politically correct. "Please speak to the Ex-DCP Headquarters", said Ranjit Gupta brusquely and hung up. But security arrangements for the Union-Minister-in transit were nevertheless made.

In 1958, at a relatively young age of 38, he was posted as

Deputy Inspector General, Northern Range. In 1960, Ranjit Gupta travelled on study leave to observe the New Scotland Yard, the West Ridings Police in Yorkshire, and the Deuxieme Bureau in Paris. On return to India, he joined as the DIG, Armed Police, Training and Border Police. He had the distinction of organizing the Border Police from scratch in West Bengal—a state which has one of the longest and most sensitive international borders in India—nearly 2,217 kilometres of frontiers with Bangladesh (then East Pakistan), about 100 kilometres with Nepal and around 185 kilometres with Bhutan. The task demanded a lot of critical thinking, planning and resourcefulness, and Ranjit Gupta truly measured up to this task. He was the DIG (Border Police) during the Indo-Pakistan War of 1965 and that made all the difference. No matter where he was posted, Ranjit Gupta invariably raised the bar, and thereby his own stature and that of the organization he was leading. Working with him was a great learning experience for the youngsters as well as the seniors. Even as OSD, Food Corporation of India in 1967, when the silos of West Bengal were almost empty, he showed his mettle as a consummate administrator who could take up any assignment. He virtually built up the Food Corporation in West Bengal, and went around Delhi and Chandigarh "with a begging bowl", and managed to get 5,000 metric tons of rice from the CM of Punjab. He had friends in all the high places and access to everyone—a positive attribute of any successful officer.

After a brief stint in the Civil Defence and another as the DIG Central Range, he was posted as the head of the Intelligence Branch in Calcutta by the United Front government in 1969. While he succeeded in bringing about some important changes in the Home Guards organization in spite of his short tenure, as DIG of the Intelligence Branch at the iconic "13, Lord Sinha Road", Ranjit Gupta dedicated himself completely to the study and monitoring of the Naxalite strategy and plans, both from their covert sources and occasionally from the intercepts of the 'directives' from the higher echelons in the organization to their foot soldiers. He also streamlined the District Intelligence Branches to the extent possible under constraints of resource crunch and the absence of any clear political mandate. He effectively brought substance and depth to the somewhat lacklustre Intelligence Branch since he understood well the goals and objectives of intelligence. The institutional knowledge thus built up by him subsequently helped the state administration while dealing with the menace of Naxalism. His experience in the 'Civil Defence' also came in handy while dealing with the "Maoist terror" as the Commissioner of Police when he deployed the "lumpen proletariat" disguised as Home Guards to provide valuable actionable intelligence.

When the Second United Front government was dismissed by the central government in March 1970, Naxalism was at its peak. Ranjit Gupta was made the Commissioner of Police, Calcutta in the face of trenchant opposition from interested quarters, with the mandate to combat the spine-chilling Naxalite terror. To quote Inder Malhotra, "the wide world was abuzz with lurid reports of the mindless Naxalite violence, what with college boys and lumpen goons killing individual policemen and Radio Peking screaming that this was the spark that would start a prairie fire". The police force, confused, demoralized and indisciplined, had to be given the backbone to fight back. "It was the job of the police force to guard the state", writes Ranjit Gupta in his rather unconventional book on the Naxalite movement, viz. *The Scarlet Agenda*, "But first, the force itself needed to learn how to guard itself." The Calcutta Police Force had been subverted by the CPI(M)–led United Front government. The CPI (M) dominated the Calcutta Police Association, a typical leftist trade union. Inder Malhotra sums up the situation admirably:" In an exquisite turn of irony, Maoists ran amuck while Marxists were ruling the state of West Bengal." P.K. Sen, the then Commissioner of Police and another illustrious officer of the West Bengal cadre, was by then dejected and dismayed because of the unending "annihilations" and there being minimal support from the effete ruling dispensation (which was soon dismissed) and decided to go on leave preparatory to retirement. Ranjit Gupta was asked to succeed him by the central government. His posting as the CP of Calcutta was opposed by many, including Sam Manekshaw, who was quoted by the then Director I.B. Madan Hooja as having told Prime Minister Indira Gandhi that "it was not a good choice, making Ranjit Gupta the Commissioner of Police in Calcutta". Ajoy Mukherjee, arguably "the most inefficient Chief Minister West Bengal had ever seen", had also written to Mrs.

Gandhi objecting to Ranjit Gupta's elevation. As CP, Calcutta, he worked directly under Govind Narain, ICS, who was the Union Home Secretary, to restore the rule of law in West Bengal.

Ranjit Gupta bravely undertook the challenge of identifying the "new votaries of an ideology of brutality, spot their hideouts and put them down"—a dilemma which another great police officer K.P.S. Gill, faced two decades later in respect of the Punjab insurgency. Ranjit Gupta relentlessly waged his war against the Extremists, first as the Commissioner of Police, and later as IGP. It is no secret that to him, ends were more important than means, and he was determined to wipe out the Crimson Terror from the state of West Bengal with courage, determination and a degree of ruthlessness. Many were critical of his methods as they were later critical of K.P.S. Gill's high-handed approach. I may be excused for this slight digression, but it would be interesting to note an uncanny coincidence and parallel between the turbulent situations in West Bengal in the 1960s and 70s and in Punjab during the 80s and 90s. Ranjit Gupta's incumbency as IGP was co-terminus with that of Siddhartha Shankar Ray (incidentally, both were born in 1920), who was Chief Minister from 1972 to 1977. Ironically, when K.P.S. Gill dealt with the challenge of insurgency in Punjab from 1988 to 1990 (his first stint as DGP), Siddhartha Shankar Ray happened to be there in his new avatar as the Governor of the state. As the Chief Minister, West Bengal, his first and immediate challenge was to subdue the Naxalite movement, though he subsequently faced charges of brutal suppression; widespread accusations of abuses by the police and the murder of youths in suspicious circumstances.

Coming back to Ranjit Gupta's narrative as CP, Calcutta, like his predecessor P.K. Sen, he too wanted to abdicate when the urban terror continued unabated. The number of depredations by the Maoists had increased manifold and there was a murderous attempt on the life of Justice T. Mukherji. Another High Court Judge, Justice K.L. Roy, had been killed by the Naxalites. Ranjit Gupta must have despaired like Hamlet:

The time is out of joint, O cursed spite,
That ever I was born to set it right.

He was candid enough to admit that his induction in the

Calcutta Police did not stop the Naxalite murders. He therefore offered to resign, but was persuaded by B.B. Ghosh, the Principal Adviser to the Governor, not out of any love for Ranjit Gupta, but because of the TINA factor. I am again reminded of Shakespeare:

There is a divinity which shapes our ends,
Rough hew them how we might.

Ranjit Gupta—Destiny's child—eventually, brought the situation in Calcutta under reasonable control. In addition to several feathers in his cap, he also had to his credit the successful and largely peaceful conduct of Assembly polls in early 1971. Thus came the Second United Front into power, but the honeymoon did not last very long. Quite often in the thick of controversy, Ranjit Gupta had trouble with the political establishment and in April 1971, he proceeded on leave.

He returned in 1972 as IG of West Bengal (then police chief; the post of Director General was yet to be created), and continued in that position till July 1976. "He was probably one of the most controversial personalities that the Calcutta or West Bengal Police have had", according to a report published in *The Times of India*. Known for his tough stance against the Naxalites in the early 70s, he was hated not only by supporters of the ultra left philosophy and human rights activists, but also by a section of mainstream politicians whose line he refused to toe. His juniors held him in high regard though, particularly for his integrity and strength of character. The greatest thing about him was that he would zealously protect those working under him once he was convinced that they had done no wrong. Perhaps no one can vouch for this better than me. In 1976, I had a problem with a prominent Minister in Siddhartha Shankar Ray's government. Although Ranjit Gupta was then busy fighting his own battles with the Administration, he gave me all the necessary advice and moral support and even arranged a private meeting for me with the Chief Minister.

Ranjit Gupta led a charmed life, and would not bother much about public opinion. An Under Secretary in Writers' Buildings once shared an interesting story which best illustrates this observation. As IGP, Ranjit Gupta had once strongly opposed a particular proposal on file that was received from the Home Department for his views. Six months later, Ranjit Gupta himself initiated the same scheme, and naturally was caught on the wrong foot by a Babu of the Home Department who sent back the file, asking the IGP to reconcile the contradiction and re-state his position. The IGP returned the file with the following note:

> *Do I contradict myself?*
> *Very well, then I contradict myself,*
> *I am large, I contain multitudes.*
> (From Walt Whitman's *Song of Myself*)

Ranjit Kumar Gupta died on May 19, 2012 at the ripe old age of 92. In his departure, we lost a person who had become a legend during his lifetime and who was a born leader of the police force, the kind of whom we would never see again. These lines from Shelley's sonnet Ozymandias well up from somewhere:-

> *Look on my works, ye Mighty, and despair!*
> *Nothing beside remains. Round the decay*
> *Of that colossal wreck, boundless and bare*
> *The lone and level sands stretch far away.*

7

My Reminiscences of Ashwini Kumar

A.P. Bhatnagar

Ashwini Kumar was posted as the Inspector General of Punjab Police in June 1971. He already held the post of Inspector General of Border Security Force, Western Borders, at the time. Everybody in Punjab was familiar with Ashwini Kumar's formidable reputation. In Punjab, he was considered to be the most dynamic police officer Punjab had seen. His leadership qualities had already become legendary. Besides, he was considered as one of the best sports administrators in the country.

I had heard about him after joining the Punjab Police, but these were just stories to me. I had never before met him or interacted with him. I was posted in Ferozepur district as an IPS Probationer for practical training and had hardly been out of Ferozepur. Therefore, it came as a surprise when, one day, I received telegraphic instructions to immediately report to the Punjab Police Headquarters at Chandigarh.

At the police headquarters, I was presented before Ashwini Kumar, IGP. He received me warmly and briefly explained that he had selected me to set up a modern control room for the police department; better than any police control room in the country. He also entrusted me the motor transport section and looking after guests of the police department, who were mostly his own guests. I was given freedom to summon any official from anywhere in Punjab to work/assist me to set up the control room at the earliest, in view of the urgency and importance of the matter. He explained that war with Pakistan appeared to be imminent, and the Punjab Police should be fully prepared to play its part. I was also asked to keep him informed of the progress of the work and I could walk into his room directly.

It soon became known to all senior officers in the PHQ that IGP had given me wide ranging powers, which, in the normal course of working, should have been the domain of his staff officers. Gradually, I realized that the IGP's. blessing had enabled me to establish myself as an important functionary of the police department, and many senior officers gave me my due.

However, it is interesting to recall how I was brought down to earth. I had started my work to set up the control room. AIG (Administration) had handed over to me maps (blueprints) of various districts of Punjab to be displayed in the control room for reference. These were not Survey of India maps; I had pointed out to AIG, while taking over, that these would not look good. However, I was advised to use only these maps as this was IGP's instruction. One morning, while I was in the office lift, on my way to the control room, the IGP also suddenly came and joined me to go to his room, which was on a different floor. He asked me how the work was progressing, and told me that he would drop in at the end of the day to check.

He walked into the control room, accompanied by virtually all the officers posted at the PHQ. As his eyes fell on the board on which a map was pinned, he lost his cool. He looked at the AIG and thundered, "Couldn't we find a better person than this nincompoop?" and sauntered out, followed by others. I was struck dumb. That night, I had a very disturbed sleep, and kept thinking about the evening incident as well as what to do.

Next morning, I visited the office of the Survey of India, where my friend's father was head of the office. I narrated to him my experience of the previous day and requested him to give me the numbers of the Survey of India maps of the districts of Punjab, and also help me in processing them. He was very helpful and gave me not only the numbers of the maps but also an introduction to the Survey of India officers in Dehradun, where the office was located.

In the afternoon, I walked into the IGP's room and sought his permission to visit Dehradun. On his asking what was the purpose of my visit, I told him I was going to Dehradun to collect the maps for the control room. He rose from his chair, took me to the corner of the room where his sofa set for receiving visitors was placed, ordered tea and told me, "Bhatnagar, I am very happy that Punjab Police has got a good officer like you. Yesterday, my irritation was not directed towards you but towards my staff officer, who had got those maps." He called the AIG and told him to give me some money which I might need. He also gave references of some BSF officers in Delhi, and asked me to visit Delhi, if I failed to get all the maps at Dehradun, and requested them to give me the maps, and also help me to procure these if some were not immediately available. I thanked him and left for Dehradun by jeep, the same evening.

A few days later, after I returned and displayed the maps on the board, he visited the control room again. He appeared to be happy with the pace and quality of work. He paid me compliments and asked whether the IGP deserved a cup of tea. I asked one of the persons working with me in the control room to quickly bring tea for all of us. However, the tea was served in the usual canteen type of cups, and some of it spilled over in the saucers. When tea was offered to Ashwini Kumar, he refused to accept it, and said, "Is this how you offer tea to your senior officers?", and immediately left the room. The AIG, who had accompanied the IGP, told me that Ashwini Kumar liked being treated like a dignitary. Therefore, I should purchase good quality crockery for my office as well and keep a few decent snacks which could be offered to him whenever he visited my office. He gave me some money for it. Accordingly, I purchased a tea-set of bone-china and some dry fruit, and started offering them to the senior officers, whenever they visited me. Ashwini Kumar specially liked the sweet, kalakand.

Shortly after this incident, after the control room had been set in order, he asked the media, which visited him almost daily, to meet me instead, to know about developments relating to the border areas. Though he was awfully busy, he always had time for me. He also found me curious about developing situations. So he would pass on to me information, which I would share with the media, and in turn, would collect many stories, and pass them on to the IGP, from time to time.

In October 1971, Ex-Army, IPS Probationers, who had joined the service with me, or one year after me, were promoted, even before completing their probation period, to head the newly created India Armed Police Battalions. Though my service record was better than theirs yet my name was not considered for promotion. Ashwini Kumar noted this omission, and inquired from the AIG about it. He told the AIG that I deserved to be promoted immediately. So my orders for promotion followed soon after. I was posted as the Deputy Commandant of a battalion, whose Commandant was an ex-Army IPS Probationer recently promoted, and who was under training with me in Ferozepur. However, Ashwini Kumar shifted me to Ludhiana as SP (Hqrs.) within weeks of my posting on promotion, when he realized this anomaly.

I used to meet Ashwini Kumar off and on in Ludhiana, whenever he happened to pass through Ludhiana. On one occasion, he suddenly asked me why most of the Naxalites in Ludhiana and of neighbouring areas wanted to surrender only to me and avoided other police officers? I didn't know the answer. However, he told my SSP that perhaps they were able to open up to me during interrogation, because I did not use third degree methods to make them talk. Ashwini Kumar had a sharp eye, and tried to know about officers serving under him. No wonder, he was a dynamic leader and took the best from his officers.

Ashwini Kumar was transferred soon after, and I did not get a chance to meet him during my and his service tenure. However, I tried to know about his abilities as a professional police officer. I did not get much information except how he led the police force in a particular situation, which only spoke about his leadership qualities. For example, he was handpicked in 1951, at a very early stage of his career, to tackle the notorious Bhupat gang in Saurashtra. Even Pt. Nehru heard about Ashwini Kumar's leadership during that time. He is also remembered for apprehending the killers of Pratap Singh Kairon, a former Chief Minister of Punjab, after a dramatic chase in Nepal. During his police career Ashwini Kumar was conferred the Padma Bhushan in 1972, the President's Police Medal for Gallantry, twice, the President's Medal for Distinguished Service and the Police Medal for Meritorious Service.

After my retirement from service, I shifted to Delhi in 2007. I was destined to meet him again in Delhi. He was then a patron of the recently formed Association of Retired Senior IPS Officers. In 2008, I was elected as Secretary of ARSIPSO. Ashwini Kumar would often go out of the way to give voluntary contributions to keep ARSIPSO activities alive. He was regular in attending functions of ARSIPSO, and very accessible to all its members. He used to keenly read articles written by its members published in newspapers, and send his comments to them. A few of them were also invited by him to social get-togethers. He maintained a good library at his home, where he regularly used to spend time reading. On one occasion, he showed me excerpts of comments written by British Police Officers in their books, about him, when he was a young police officer in Punjab.

He was fond of reminiscing about his time spent as a police officer, and often narrated anecdotes about those times. I recall, at the felicitation ceremony organized by ARSIPSO in his honour, he told the participants how he had escorted trains full of refugees during partition.

Ashwani Kumar was fond of the good things in life—music, literature, painting, poetry, good food and good company. He was the patron of many institutions promoting such activities. Annual music sammelan—Harballabh music festival—was one such event he patronized.

The narrative will be incomplete without mentioning his passion for sports. He recruited many hockey players and other sportsmen in the Punjab Police and the BSF, who later became renowned international players. One of my colleagues (from MP) once narrated a fascinating account of his passion for hockey. The BSF (or perhaps Punjab) team was defeated by the team from MP. Ashwini Kumar spent the entire time after the game with the defeated team. The MP team's captain (K.P. Singh, who later became DIB) ultimately walked up to Ashwini Kumar to seek his blessings for the victorious team. It is only then that Ashwini Kumar could be separated from his team.

Ashwini Kumar headed many sports bodies. However, his favourite sport was hockey. He presided over the Indian Hockey Federation and was also the Vice-President of the International Olympic Association. He was later honoured by making him a Life Member of the International Olympic Association.

Recently, there was a strong censure, in the media, of senior police officers by Delhi policemen, for not standing up with the police force after some police personnel were assaulted in a Delhi Court premises by some errant lawyers. My thoughts immediately raced back to Ashwini Kumar about whom it was said that policemen in Punjab were always prepared to give their lives for him.

8

Imdad Ali

Biswakesh Tripathy

Imdad Ali belonged to an aristocratic family of Assam. He joined as an IP Officer in 1938 and belonged to the Assam cadre. He joined CRPF as DG in 1969. I have worked under him as Commandant posted at Calcutta (as it was then known) during the height of Naxalite depredations in Calcutta and other places in West Bengal. Though it was a very tense situation for the CRPF, he, as DG of

CRPF, never got flustered. He was always calm and collected. He never lost his temper, or shouted at anyone. He calmly analysed each situation and gave proper directions. I have seen very few officers of such an even temperament like him.

He and his wife were of an aristocratic breed. Their language and deportment were always chaste. He often used to invite his junior colleagues for an evening of cocktails and dinner. He and his wife were fond of whisky and both smoked. It was a rare sight in those days to find a lady, that too a Muslim lady, drinking and smoking and talking to men on equal terms. On such evenings, Mr. Ali used to talk a lot for which his wife gibed at him by saying "old, therefore, garrulous." We used to have a good laugh at the cost of Mr. Ali, who enjoyed his wife's banter. They were a loving couple.

Imdad Ali was also an affectionate person. When I was posted as DIG CRPF at Poona (1970-73), he visited Poona for inspection. He learnt that my son was very ill. In spite of his heavy schedule of work, he made it a point to come to my house to look up my ailing son, and give courage to my wife.

There was one Commandant in CRPF called Maha Singh. He was an SI in the Haryana Armed Police. He joined CRPF on deputation as an Inspector. He earned his promotions from time to time and became a Commandant. He was a sincere and honest officer and an affectionate man. After retirement, he contested the Assembly elections from Gurgaon in Haryana and was easily elected. He was popular in Gurgaon as he had recruited a number of persons as constables from various villages of Gurgaon while he was a Commandant in CRPF. He was popularly known as Col Maha Singh in Gurgaon. Bhajan Lal, the then Chief Minister of Haryana, appointed him as a cabinet minister. An SI of Haryana police became a cabinet minister—a rare achievement.

While in CRPF, serving as a Commandant, he had worked under many officers. He had worked with me as a Commandant while I was also a Commandant. When I was promoted as a DIG, he worked under me, but we continued as dear colleagues. When I was DIG, posted at Delhi, Maha Singh was a minister in Haryana. At times, he came to Delhi on work and stayed in Haryana Bhawan. In the evenings, he used to come to my official residence. He would stand to attention and salute me, as if I was his senior police officer. I would embrace him. He would then request me for a drink. He could not take alcohol at Haryana Bhawan, and that was why, he used to come to my house, whenever possible. I would gladly give him rum, which was our favourite drink. Though he was a minister, he respected me as his senior in police.

In those days, the annual conference of CRPF was held at Neemuch, which was attended by all the officers from DG to Commandant. In 1974, we had all assembled at Neemuch for the conference. Maha Singh decided to visit us there, though he was not invited. His intention was to come quietly and meet a few old friends, and go back to Delhi. But when the unexpected news of his visit came, there was a lot of confusion among us. Maha Singh had served under all the DIGs, IGs and the DG as a subordinate, and he was saluting all these officers. Now he was coming as an Hon'ble Minister. How should he be received? All that time, Mr. Imdad Ali was the DG. He ended the confusion by saying Maha Singh should be received as an Hon'ble Minister, and all officers, right from the Commandant to DG must salute him, and give him due respect as a minister. We, the senior officers, led by the DG, Imdad Ali, stood in front of the officers' mess. When the Hon'ble Minister came to the mess, Imdad Ali called everyone to attention, and gave a smart salute. Some of us, like me, who were close to Maha Singh while he was in CRPF, tried our best to suppress our smile. However, Imdad Ali, with proper courtesy, escorted the Hon'ble Minister to the officers' mess, requested him to take a seat, and offered him a cold drink. I could see Maha Singh was feeling extremely uncomfortable in the presence of Mr. Ali and other senior officers whom he was saluting the other day.

He soon signed the visitor's Book, which was a formality, and requested me to take him to the room where I was staying. As soon as he entered my room, he came to attention and gave me a smart salute. I embraced him. He said he had come to Neemuch to meet all his friends and erstwhile colleagues. But he did not know it would be such an embarrassing experience. He felt extremely awkward when such a senior officer as DG, CRPF called all the officers to attention and saluted him. I told him to relax. That was the proper thing to do since he had come as a minister. I also told him we were proud of him as he had become a minister. Imdad Ali also said so. This shows the humility of Maha Singh, though he had become a minister. This also shows Imdad Ali's clarity of mind about observing the proper protocol for a minister, even if he had once been his subordinate.

After retirement in the year 1973, Mr. Ali was posted as India's ambassador to UAE. It was a rare honour for a police officer. He joined there as ambassador. But unfortunately, his wife was afflicted with cancer, for which he gave up the prize post and returned to India for better treatment of his wife. Mrs. Ali died of cancer at Delhi. I, along with some others of his family and friends, attended her burial. I remember to have held a fistful of earth that I threw into her grave with tears in my eyes. Imdad Ali became a widower and a retired person around the age of sixty. He was lonely and sad. But, after a few days, he put it behind him, and started a new life. He used to stay in a room in Delhi Gymkhana, and made the Gymkhana his new home. He lived an active club life with a few friends, and spent his time. Imdad Ali is remembered and admired by all who knew and worked with him. He was the personification of courtesy and civility, and captivated everyone by his grace and dignity.

9

R.K. Padhi

Amiya Bhusan Tripathy

He left the world three years before his retirement, at the age of 55, at the peak of his career, leaving not only the members of the Orissa Police sad, shocked and shedding tears, but also the people of Orissa, in general, and his native place Parlakhimedi, a town in South Orissa, in particular. Professional competence apart, he had become an eminent public figure in the state, an intellectual of a very high order, an educationist, bubbling with ideas, and a social reformist, within the parameters of a police career. Thus, describing the man R.K. Padhi means delving into his multifaceted personality that placed him in an iconic position in the Orissa Police.

Born into a police family on January 25, 1919, his father, Binayak Padhi, had retired as an Inspector of Police in the erstwhile Madras Presidency; he was the eldest of ten children, eight brothers and two sisters. He showed flashes of brilliance, right from his childhood. Starting his school education in one of the rural schools in the Telugu-speaking Andhra area, he topped the SSLC (Matriculation) examination. He studied Intermediate Science in Vishakhapatnam and secured three gold medals in Physics, Chemistry, and Mathematics. In 1937, he joined Ravenshaw College at Cuttack, switching over to Arts in the BA with English Honours. He was adjudged the best debater in 1938 and won similar laurels in Calcutta in the Eastern India debate competition. After topping the merit list in the BA Honours examination, he proceeded to Patna to do his MA in English, but the financial position in his family, with nine brothers and sisters, did not allow him to proceed with his studies, forcing him to return to Orissa in search of a job, to supplement the family income.

In search of a job, he met the late L.P. Singh of the ICS, then Collector, Cuttack, who later became the Union Home Secretary. Impressed with his academic credentials and impressive personality, L.P. Singh helped him get the job of a Deputy Collector, in which capacity he was posted at Bhadrak at the tender age of 21. That was only a mile post; he prepared for the Indian Police (IP) examinations in 1941, and topped the list of successful candidates, with a record of securing 400 marks out of 400 in the personality test, and 87 per cent in English literature, setting in motion an eventful and distinguished career.

R.K. Padhi was allotted the combined Bihar and Orissa cadre, and after his basic training in the Police Training College at Hazaribagh, he started performing police duties as Asst. Superintendent of Police at Jamalpur in Bihar. Those days, the term Asst. Superintendent of Police was more commonly used than Subdivisional Police Officer. He was subsequently posted as ASP, Bhanjnagar, then called Russelkonda, one of the oldest subdivisions in Orissa in the southern district of Ganjam. He also served as the Superintendent of Police, Puri district, and ADC to three Governors of Orissa - Sir Chandulal Trivedi of the ICS, Kailash Nath Katju and Asaf Ali from 1946 to 1951. He had the distinction of being appointed as the Honorary ADC to the President of India, which was a rare honour.

He went on deputation to the Government of India to the Intelligence Bureau as Assistant Director, and served under the first Director T.G. Sanjivi Pillay of the erstwhile Madras cadre and witnessed the legendary B.N. Mullick taking over as Director, after Sanjivi was repatriated to Madras. Because of family problems, he was posted at Cuttack as the Central Intelligence Officer. On repatriation to Orissa, he was promoted to the rank of DIG of police, at an early age. He served as the DIG of the undivided Central Range, which covered the coastal districts of Cuttack - Puri, Balasore and the former princely state of Mayurbhanj. He was also the DIG, CID and Railways, which included the Crime Branch, Intelligence and Railways.

Professionally competent, integrity beyond question, and with a mind for the welfare of the force, R.K. Padhi became the darling of the officers and men. What was officer R.K. Padhi, as a man, and what made him so special? As a man, he demonstrated several qualities ingrained in him from his childhood. Coming from a middle class background, he never lost his moorings, even after joining the covetous service of the IP Humility was his forte, and as he climbed the ladder in the service, humanism and empathy were abundantly in evidence in his work and dealings. He used to say that he was proud, proud of the service, to which he belonged, for, according to him, the police was the best public service. With a commanding personality, he firmly believed in developing the leadership qualities of the IPS and OPS officers. He was never afraid, never indulged in double speaking, never crawled and bowed before the powers that be, and followed these cardinal principles to the end of his life. For this, he suffered in his career, but never grumbled and made an issue. He would walk from one job to another, with effortless ease. Luxury was anathema to him, members of his large family led a very simple and frugal life.

Usually dressed in simple attire, like trousers and half bush shirt, he allowed himself three luxuries, coffee at 11 am, smoking cigarettes, which he loved to roll, and drinking, the then popular Indian brand whisky, Blacknight, in the Cuttack Club, never longing for Scotch. Intellectually, he was a class unto himself, then virtually unheard of in the bureaucracy in Orissa. Brilliant in English, and, as an orator, he was a prolific reader, speaking in his inimitable style, not only to the police officers, but also in other forums like public meetings, colleges, universities and other institutions, holding his audience in thrall. I am highlighting some of the basic traits of his personality, which blossomed and peaked when he took the reins of the Orissa Police, and made him an iconic figure.

That was the time when the State Road Transport system was controlled by the government and headed by a Transport Controller. R.K. Padhi has served in this post in various capacities like DIG, Additional IG and later as IG. When it was converted to a Corporation, he was the first Chairman of the Corporation. He headed the State Vigilance and Anti-Corruption organization and it was in 1964-65 that I first came into contact with him. Prior to that it was only a mandatory official call along with my batchmates. While heading the Vigilance organization, he displayed fairplay, impartiality, and believed in transparency. Zealously, protecting the pride in the service, he would brook no compromise in upholding the dignity of a post. Those days the police, though the most important and visible arm of the government, did not get the due it deserved. In the Order of Precedence, the DIG was bracketed with a Deputy Secretary, while officers in the senior scale in the IAS were holding the post of Secretaries in the state. Army Brigadiers were privileged to remain in that serial. At a state function, the IP DIG, R.K. Padhi, seeing himself in that order, refused to stand in line, and took up the matter with the government for upgrading the DIG to the serial where Secretaries to the government and Army Brigadiers were placed. And it was done.

In early 1967, the first non-Congress coalition ministry was formed, with the late R.N. Singhdeo of the Ganatantra Parishad, a regional outfit, which subsequently merged with the Swatantra party, as the Chief Minister, with the support of Dr. Harekrushna Mahtab, the first Congress Chief Minister after independence, who had formed another regional party, called Jana Congress. This heralded a change in the police leadership, and R.K. Padhi was the inevitable choice. He rose to the occasion, and after taking over as the Inspectoral General of Police, at the age of 48, he sent a highly inspirational message to the officers and men, which, as far as I remember, started with—"On taking over the command of the Orissa Police, I send my greetings to----". This very message from the Police Chief created great excitement and anticipation in the force. We, the junior officers, many of us who were vocal, rejoiced.

Two immediate steps taken by him won him laurels not only from the police force, but also from the public, establishing his credentials as a visionary. The first was aimed at creating an identity for the Orissa Police, that would set it apart from other departments, that was celebration of the Orissa Police Formation Day on 1st April of every year. This was the day when a separate province for the Oriya-speaking people was formed in 1936. The celebration included morning parade in each district and battalion headquarters, meetings involving members of public during the day and Badakhana for the force, at night, accompanied by entertainment programmes. This was a trendsetter, for, what to speak of other major departments, there was no celebration at the state level. Several years later the state government decided to follow the police, and now the State Formation Day, called Utkal Divas, is being observed.

The second was the introduction of the Inter Battalion Competition, every two years to promote the operational efficiency of the force, and develop the spirit of camaraderie. At that time, there were only six battalions, and logistically, it was possible to organize the event. And it was during one of his tenures as Police Chief, he asked me (I had joined as his Staff Officer) to prepare a proposal for a new battalion at Bhubaneswar, took the proposal by hand to Bhubaneswar, and got the sanction of the Governor. That was during a spell of the Governor's rule.

Talking about his principled stand, let me narrate two events concerning me, which had a long term effect on the police department, which enhanced his image, endearing him to everyone. I was ADC to the Governor of Orissa, M.A. Ansari in 1967. For various reasons, I fell out with the Governor, who sent two signed cryptic notes, one to the government, that my services were dispensed with, and the post of Police ADC would be abolished, and a more humiliating note to his Secretary, a perfect gentleman, to instruct the Raj Bhawan guard not to allow me entry to the Raj Bhawan. The Home Secretary, who, for various reasons, had taken a dislike to me, was ready to implement the order. R.K. Padhi was camping at Rourkela. Hearing the news from the Home Secretary, with whom he was barely on speaking terms, and had vowed not to enter his room till the departure of the incumbent, he rang me from Rourkela, and heard the details. Next morning, when I entered Raj Bhawan, in spite of the prohibitory order of the Governor, the Secretary called me, and showed a wireless message from R.K. Padhi to the Governor, which started with the words, "Deeply aggrieved with the decision of the Governor to shift ADC A.B. Tripathy—", and whose gist was, while he could change the person, he could not wind up the post. The post remained with the police, and I was transferred as SP, Mayurbhanj.

The second instance was much more significant. I had a difference of opinion with the Collector, and the government, in their wisdom (propelled by the Home Secretary), decided to shift me. Here, again, R.K. Padhi intervened, not on my behalf, but as a matter of principle. He wrote strongly to the government that in the district administration, the DM and SP function as a team, and if there is any remiss, both are responsible, and should be transferred. Chief Minister, R.N. Singhdeo concurred with R.K. Padhi, and ordered the transfer of the DM.

While I was SP, Mayurbhanj, he visited Baripada. Reaching there, in the evening, he told me that he would visit one outpost, the only Police Station, and then the DPO. All three visits the next day were not fault finding, but ennobling and enabling. Police resources in those days were scanty, and the main challenge of the leader was to keep the spirit of the men high. And that was what he exactly did. In the DPO, while going through the Crime Directory, he explained the nuances and semantics of each column. Not that, I did not know about them, but what he said in his typical manner, was revealing. This example of his erudition reminds me of what P.C. Hota, an IAS officer of the Orissa cadre, belonging to my batch, who was posted as District Magistrate, Balasore, told me. Before proceeding to Balasore, he went to call on R.K. Padhi, and when he left, his mind was surcharged with thoughts on the advice and instructions he received. P.C. Hota retired as the Chairman of the UPSC.

R.K. Padhi's first term as IGP, Orissa, was predictably linked to J.C. Ghosh's, the seniormost police officer in the state, reinstatement as the Police Chief. Chief Minister R.N. Singhdeo, a fair minded person, had written to the Home Ministry to expunge some unfavourable remarks, which stood in his way. The remarks were expunged, and the Chief Minister appointed J.C. Ghosh as the IGP. This was where R.K. Padhi showed his true greatness. Before handing over, he flashed a message, which started like this: "In a few hours from now, I shall be handing over the command of the Orissa Police to our former Chief, J.C. Ghosh, I.P. etc.", no remorse, no regret, only the splendour of his personality. J.C. Ghosh, however, remained in the post for three to four months, and took long leave, preceding his retirement. And R.K. Padhi was back in the chair.

It was nearly a two-year term during which he came to be loved for his humanism, adored for his brilliance as an intellectual and feared for his outspokenness. The annual police conferences of 1968 and 69, the annual shooting meets at Dhenkanal, used to be forums where he was at his dazzling best. He would provide ample space to the young officers, and we constituted the bulk, to speak, to voice dissent, and differ, and like a benevolent patriarch, he would articulate everyone's view. I remember at one conference, where Chief Minister R.N. Singhdeo was present, he said: "My Superintendents of Police (mark the words) are worked up due to various problems plaguing the police." Dinners used to be roaring affairs with pre and post-dinner bonhomie abundantly in evidence.

It is not that R.K. Padhi had smooth sailing during the period. In the top echelons, rivalry, undercutting, intolerance and the accompanying factors, mainly political, were, and continue to be the bane of the department. J.C. Ghosh IP, for whom he had great respect, S.K. Ghosh, an IPS officer, one of the most powerful Police Chiefs Orissa had from 1964 to 1967, whom he replaced, and B.B. Mishra IP, who was Inspectoral General in the CRPF, were his seniors. J.C Ghosh, while on leave, was once returning from Calcutta to Cuttack by car, and wanted to have lunch at Baripada, where I was SP. At that time, an agitation engineered by some vested interests over an alleged act of misconduct of some IPS officers, and fanned by a newspaper owned by a powerful politician, was in the last stage. In the Circuit House, while we were discussing various matters, J.C. Ghosh told me, "Tripathy, so long as (so and so, referring to a particular officer) is there, R.K. will not have a peaceful time." Even after the agitation, the newspaper continued the charade, creating a piquant situation for R.N. Singhdeo, whose party was in coalition with the party headed by Harekrushna Mahtab, founder of the newspaper. With the likely return of B.B. Mishra in the second half of 1969 from the Centre, the exit of R.K. Padhi was written on the wall. But he was not worried in the least, and conducted the affairs of the department with exemplary enthusiasm. I will cite two instances, which will testify to this and indicate his thought level.

In July 1969, the famous Nabakalebara festival was held in Puri. This festival is celebrated in the year in which two Asadhas (month) fall when the wooden Bigrahas of the three deities— Jagannath, Balabhadra and Subhadra—are replaced with new ones, and the Daru Brahma transferred from the old ones to the new. This is followed by the Ratha Yatra (annual car festival). Because of this significance, lakhs of pilgrims from all over India throng to Puri, for which large scale police arrangements are made for the festival. At that time, N.K. Singh of the 1961 batch was SP, Puri, and Narsingh Swain of the 1950 batch, who became Police Chief in 1974, was the DIG Central range. R.K. Padhi drafted three IPS officers of the rank of Superintendent of Police to manage the festival along with N.K. Singh. I was one, the other two were B.B. Panda and B.P. Saha, both of the 1963 batch. And of course junior IPS officers were drafted. While I was in charge of crime control and allied matters, B.P. Saha was in charge of traffic control. B.B. Panda remained in charge of logistics and camps. Narsingh Swain and R.K. Padhi were always there. The entire festival passed off smoothly but, for an incident, in which the car of Lord Jagannath, while being dragged, hit a building, causing some damage. The Nabakalebara festival is a major challenge to the police and the senior officers in charge keep their fingers crossed till the completion of all rites and rituals. It fell next in 1977, and then in 1996, when I was DG Police.

Volunteering to go on leave to allow the next person to hold the highest post is unthinkable at present. It was only R.K. Padhi, who could do that not once but twice. In January 1969, he went on leave so that H.P. Singh Deo, the next senior most, remained in charge of the post before his retirement. He again went on leave in March to enable James Dharmaraj to hold the office before proceeding to CBI as Joint Director. These are gestures which show the man for what he is as a leader, a colleague and an officer and R.K. Padhi exhibited them in ample measure.

B.B. Mishra IP, on return from the Centre, took over as Police Chief in August 1969, and R.K. Padhi became the Head of the State Vigilance organization. He never avoided a single function or meeting during the tenure of B.B. Mishra, and gave him full respect in all functions, though he was only a year junior to him. During this period, I changed places thrice. I went to Keonjhar as SP at the beginning of 1970, then to Cuttack as Commandant of the first OMP Battalion mid-1971, and then to Berhampur in October 1971 as SP Vigilance southern division. The Home Secretary, who was ill-disposed towards me, had communicated an adverse ACR entry to me for the period when I was SP Mayurbhanj, in spite of R.K. Padhi as Police Chief countering the adverse remarks, as he told me later. Battered, I wanted to get out of the police for some time. I met R.K. Padhi, and requested him to take me to Vigilance. He was not only sympathetic but promised to take me to Vigilance in the next vacancy which occurred in October when Sankar Sen, SP of the southern division was deputed to IB.

B.B. Mishra had a fairly smooth tenure till the end of 1972 when he proceeded to the Centre as Director General, CRPF, handing over the reins to R.K. Padhi, who became Orissa Police Chief for the third time, with Congress in power, and Nandini Satpathy, a favourite of Prime Minister Indira Gandhi, as Chief Minister. Even at that stage, he had a clear four years to go. At that time, the shenanigans of a very senior police officer, who was suffering from a persecution complex, and had targeted Police Chiefs like S.K. Ghosh, B.B. Mishra and R.K. Padhi, were creating an uneasy atmosphere in the police. His activities peaked during B.B Mishra's time, and continued unabated. I was a witness to his open defiance of R.K. Padhi at Berhampur, Headquarters of the Range DIG where he called a meeting of all SPs of the Range. This officer, as SP of a district, not only did not attend, but also managed a wireless message sent to the IGP camp, Berhampur, by the District Magistrate, to the effect that the SP was not in a position to leave the district because of the law and order situation. This incident obviously set R.K. Padhi on a course to take some stiff measures. By that time, Padmanav Mishra had become the Home Secretary and R.K. Padhi entered the Home Secretary's room after a long gap. The Home Secretary was a gentleman, friendly and positive thinking. He also became another target of the SP on the rampage. The situation exploded when the SP got a case registered against the Home Secretary in a police station in his district under corruption-related laws. The state was agog with news, which would have a far-reaching effect on the discipline and morale of the force. R.K. Padhi felt hurt, wounded and let down. Being a man, even-tempered and articulate, he lost his cool, and reprimanded the IPS officers at a meeting by saying, "I am ashamed of leading a cadre like yours." I was SP, Vigilance at Berhampur. He rang me, rebuked me, and asked me to join as his AIG, immediately. For me, it was a pleasure, for, I thought that I would work for my boss for three years, but alas, it would not even last for three months. The errant officer's service was terminated under Article 311 of the Constitution.

I joined as his Staff Officer in November 1973. On hand was the All India Police Duty Meet to be organized at Cuttack. S.K. Chatterjee of the 1964 batch, another AIG, was already functioning as the Organizing Secretary. He asked me to extend all help to Chatterjee to make the meet a success. Funds were limited, the grant by the government was inadequate, but with all these constraints, the meet was a success, with a parting dinner, where R.K. Padhi exuding warmth, gave his Sayonara address. Two more important landmarks, I wish to mention as they had a far-reaching effect on the police. The Sixth Finance Commission, which was in place at that time, and had mooted the idea of upgradation in the standards of administration, particularly in the regulatory departments, which generally came in the non-plan sector, was scheduled to come to Orissa, and hold discussions. R.K. Padhi asked us to prepare a note justifying inclusion of the police in the scheme, with particular reference to the Orissa Police. We prepared a note, and with that, he attended the meeting with the Commission, and on return, told us that inclusion of the police had been accepted, in principle. This was good news and the arrangement continued till the 13th Finance Commission.

Another important development that marked his openness to ideas was police housing. At that time, there was a centrally sponsored scheme, called the police Housing Scheme, in which the Centre used to provide an annual grant to the states. There used to be a Police Housing Committee under the chairmanship of the IGP, with Secretaries Home, Finance and PWD as members, and AIG (Finance) as the Secretary, and this Committee used to decide the allotment of funds. At that time, the Police Housing Corporation formed in Andhra Pradesh was creating news by launching ambitious schemes in Police Housing. At one of the meetings, I mooted the idea of studying the scheme, and this found ready acceptance. Subsquently, during the tenure of Narayan Chand as IGP, I went to Hyderabad to study the scheme, in detail.

R.K. Padhi, apart from his professional work, was associated with several cultural and social organizations in Orissa. One such organization was Rotary, of which he was an active and leading member. In January 1974, the Rotary district, which then comprised Orissa, Bihar and Madhya Pradesh, had its annual conference at Gopalpur-on-Sea, on the 19th. He was elected Governor, and, after dinner and celebrations, returned to his uncle's house at Berhampur, and retired to sleep, never to wake up again. Cruel hands of destiny snatched him away in the early hours of the 20th, leaving the Orissa Police stunned and orphaned.

I was at Bhubaneswar when I received the news from P.C. Ratho, then SP, CBI, and drove my car to Cuttack, in a dazed and stunned mind. When I arrived, I saw a tearful crowd, many weeping. I went to the room of AIG (Adm), and found many officers. Narayan Chand, his friend and next in seniority, looking vacant, overtaken with grief. He asked us to draft a condolence message, which was a Herculean task, for the heart was choked with emotions, and the mind was blank. The government had decided to accord state honours to this distinguished son of Orissa. The family members decided to take the mortal remains to Parlakhimedi. The district administration made the necessary arrangement for the same. Mr. Agnihotri, then Deputy Director ARC, provided a helicopter for some of us to go to his native town to take part in the cremation. When we reached Parlakhimedi, we saw the main road and all the streets filled with crowds, who were waiting for the last darshan of their beloved son. Collector F.A. Moses, and SP V. Apparao, were finding it difficult to steer the vehicle to the destination.

A life at the pinnacle of glory, yet to be lived in full, had come to an end. A leader loved by his men and officers, an officer standing tall in the administration, respected by politicians and colleagues alike, an intellectual par excellence, and, last, but not the least, a man with compassion and humanism, the many splendoured, R.K. Padhi left the world, leaving a legacy, whose fragrance still endures.

10

Girish Chandra (Garry) Saxena

K.M. Singh

A doyen of the police fraternity, Girish Chandra Saxena joined the Indian Police Service in 1950 and was allotted Uttar Pradesh Cadre. An accomplished intelligence officer and a security strategist, he was endowed with deep insight and knowledge of issues relating to national security and intelligence.

Born at Agra in 1928, Mr. Saxena had his schooling at Kanpur.

Intermediate from Queen's College, Varanasi, and Bachelor of Arts degree from University of Allahabad, he obtained his post-graduate degree in History, also from Allahabad University.

Girish Saxena joined the Indian Police Service in 1950. He was assigned to the Uttar Pradesh cadre, where he served as the Superintendent of Police in various districts, including Rampur, Aligarh, Bareilly and Allahabad. In 1969, he joined the Research & Analysis Wing (R&AW) in the Cabinet Secretariat in the Government of India. He headed the R&AW as Secretary from 1983 to 1986. He was the Chief of the R&AW during the Kanishka Bombing and Operation Blue Star in 1984. Under his guidance, R&AW is known to have supplied the Canadian police, the warning of a threat to Air India jets by Khalistani extremists, who were plotting to place "time-delay devices in the aircraft or registered baggage". However, security was not enhanced, leading to the blowing up of an Air India flight from Toronto via Montreal, killing all 329 on board in 1985. Along with his successors, S.E. Joshi and A.K. Verma, Saxena was among the R&AW chiefs, who played a key role in the operations of CIT-X, a covert-action unit which acted against Pakistan's backing of Khalistani terrorists.

My first meeting with him was in his office at R&AW when I was a Deputy Director in IB and Staff Officer to the then DIB, R.K. Kapoor. I had gone to meet him on the direction of the DIB to seek some help in connection with an intelligence operation in 1984. I was deeply impressed with his unassuming mannerisms and warmth with which he made me comfortable in his office. His response to our request was very positive and spontaneous. During this period, I had occasion to witness the interaction between the two Intelligence Chiefs from close quarters, being the Staff Officer of the DIB. Both, R.K. Kapoor and G.C. Saxena had studied together in Allahabad University. In the IPS, both of them were batchmates as well as cadre mates (UP). Both had a lot in common in their temperament, with suave manners and large hearts. They had an excellent rapport with tremendous mutual goodwill. When I look back, I feel that 1983 and 1984 were the golden years of excellent cooperation between the two intelligence organizations. On retirement, he remained as Advisor to the then Prime Minister, Rajiv Gandhi, for two years till 1988. His main areas of specialization were international affairs, national security and intelligence matters.

He was appointed the Governor of Jammu and Kashmir at a very critical juncture in May 1990, when the entire Kashmir valley was in turmoil following the assassination of Mirwaiz Maulvi Farooq by the militants of the Hizbul Mujahideen. He had succeeded Mr. Jagmohan, who quit owning moral responsibility for civilian killings which had taken place during the funeral procession of the Mirwaiz. Amidst this crisis situation and mass upsurge, his focus was on winning the hearts of the people. He had a very successful tenure as the Governor of J&K, and was credited with revival of the state polices' intelligence apparatus in the light of his long experience in the field of intelligence.

Mr. Saxena was a perfect embodiment of polite manners, with firm conviction and uncompromising principles. A memorable display of his mettle was evident in the second week of March 1993, when he quietly packed up his things from Raj Bhawan in Jammu, flew to Delhi, and called on the PMO to say that he was not going back. His courageous decision caused a slight constitutional crisis as the state was under Governor's rule at that time. He took this stand as he was not willing to be pushed around, or humiliated, even though he made no public statement, whatsoever.

It is a testimony to his calibre and professionalism that despite having caused a mini-constitutional crisis by leaving abruptly, he was reappointed as the Governor of the same state five years later in 1998. In his second tenure, his focus was on the revival of local intelligence and the state police, which was hitherto not on the forefront of counter-insurgency operations. During this tenure, he was lauded for his efforts, which turned the state police into an effective counter-insurgency force. "No militancy can be fought without the involvement of the local police" was his constant refrain.

During his second tenure as the Governor in J&K, G.C. Saxena headed the Committee on reforming the Indian intelligence apparatus. The other members of the Committee were the former Foreign Secretary, K. Raghunath, former IB Chief, M.K. Narayanan, former Special Secretary, MHA, P.P. Shrivastava, former R&W Special Secretary, B. Raman and R. Narsimhan of the National

Institute of Advanced Studies. The meticulously researched report calls on India's intelligence establishment to take "an honest and in-depth stock of their present intelligence effort and capabilities to meet challenges and problems." It recommended a massive upgrading of technical, imaging, signal, electronic counter-intelligence and economic intelligence capabilities and a system-wide reform of conventional human-intelligence gathering. The report was accepted by the Group of Ministers, who released their recommendations in February 2001. However, the suggestions made by the G.C. Saxena Committee on reforming the Indian intelligence apparatus remained unimplemented, reportedly in the face of bureaucratic resistance and lack of political enthusiasm.

I had the good fortune to work with him closely between 2000 to 2002 during my posting in IB at Srinagar. I used to visit the Raj Bhawan generally once a week to brief the Governor. My briefing was not more than 15-20 minutes but the meetings used to invariably last over an hour. At every meeting, I used to be a beneficiary of his long experience in the field of intelligence, and long tenure as Governor, J&K.

According to Sudhir Bloeria, an IAS Officer of the J&K cadre, G.C. Saxena was one of the best Governors that the state had seen. Bloeria was the Principal Secretary to the Governor in both the tenures of Mr. Saxena. Reflecting on his tenure in Raj Bhawan, Bloria mentioned that because of his long intelligence background, Mr. Saxena was always very circumspect and cautious at every step. He used to advise Bloeria to avoid saying anything important on the phone. He would always prefer talking in person, and if the issue was very important, he would avoid talking to Bloeria even in his office, and take him out to the lawn, or the garden outside. On one occasion, he requested Bloeria to meet an important visitor on his behalf. On being asked about the reason for the same, he told Bloeria that he wanted to avoid meeting this visitor as he knew him by his pseudo-name.

In one of my meetings at Raj Bhawan, Mr. Saxena recalled an interesting incident of his first tenure as Governor of J&K. He mentioned that a British Parliamentary delegation visiting India had come to Srinagar. They were invited at Raj Bhawan for a meeting, followed by lunch. At the end of the meeting, a member of the delegation told G.C. Saxena that he was trying to recall where he had met him as his face looked familiar. Mr. Saxena denied having ever met him earlier. The MP, however, insisted that they had met and added that he was trying to recollect. After lunch, he came to Mr. Saxena and told him that he had been able to recollect, and asked whether he was Mr. Modwell who was posted in the Indian High Commission, London, where he had met him. Mr. Saxena immediately covered up by saying that he was possibly confusing him with his brother, named Modwell, who resembled him posted in the Indian High Commission, London, long ago.

G.C. Saxena was awarded the civilian honour of Padma Bhushan in 2005.

Mr. Saxena died on April 14, 2017 after a brief illness. Talking to the PTI after his death, his brother, Naresh Chandra mentioned that "he was deeply committed even at this age about the developments and happenings in Jammu & Kashmir." He recalled that ten days ago his brother (Garry Saxena), while being wheeled out from the Intensive Care Unit (ICU) of a private hospital, had held the hand of the doctor, and said, "I don't have any stress other than the happenings in Jammu & Kashmir."

Former J&K Chief Ministers Farooq and Omar Abdullah condoled his death, saying that in his departure, a visionary had gone. "I recall my association with Governor Saxena. He was very cool in extreme situations and always had a humane approach to any problem," said Farooq Abdullah. Omar Abdullah said, "It is sad news for me. He (Saxena) had always guided me during my initial days in politics."

In her condolence message, the then Chief Minister, Mehbooba Mufti described G.C. Saxena as an able administrator, who left an indelible mark in the state during his gubernatorial assignments. In his death, the ARSIPSO lost a father figure for the Association, and the Indian Police Service, one of its brightest stars.

11

B.S. Das: An Inspiring Leader

Sankar Sen

There are some people who remain forever young and inspiring. Age does not wither or stale their physical and mental faculties. On the other hand, with advance in age, they become more gracious, positive and proactive. B.S. Das, one of the seniormost members of the Indian Police Service, is a wonderful and inspiring specimen of this rare breed. I first met him at a meeting of the Association of Senior Retired Indian Police Service Officers (ARSIPSO) in Delhi. He was one of the guiding spirits behind the formation of the Association for promoting professional deliberations among the retired police and security professionals and facilitating social intercourse among the families of the same fraternity.

Shri Das has had a chequered and successful service career. He joined the Indian Police Service in its first batch in 1948 and was allotted to the UP cadre. He held a few important and challenging charges. He was a successful Superintendent of Police of some trouble-prone districts and left his mark, wherever he was posted. He commanded the loyalty of the subordinates and won affection of the members of the public by his amiable and civilized behaviour and leadership qualities. His seniors liked him for his professionalism and commitment and juniors admired him for his magnanimity and charismatic leadership. But his indomitable and adventurous mind was looking yonder and gazing at a newer and wider horizon. He yearned for a different life and wanted to step out into a wider world.

He went on deputation to the Indian Foreign Service and commenced an altogether new but very successful innings. He served in London, Moscow and later on as Indian Ambassador in Bhutan. Subsequently, he held the challenging job of the Managing Director of Air India.

In his recently published autobiographical narrative *Memoirs of an Indian Diplomat,* Das narrates his roller-coaster ride and mentions how he had to carry the cross because of his police background. He was viewed sometimes as a *persona non-grata* and some of the stalwarts of the Indian Foreign Service, initially cold shouldered him, but later on came to appreciate the sterling qualities of his head and heart, and reposed full trust in him. He was posted as the Indian Special Officer in Bhutan and Chief Administrator, Sikkim, and displayed diplomatic skill of a high order. In Bhutan, he made a name for himself as a very successful diplomat and earned respect from all quarters. His son-in-law, Alok Prasad, a former member of the Indian Foreign Service, writes that during his visit to Bhutan in 1982, accompanying the Foreign Secretary, he was overwhelmed by high praise and affection with which everybody, including the young King, spoke about Ambassador Das. He was held in high esteem because of his high credibility and commitment.

He also had a stormy innings as the Managing Director, Air

India during the Emergency and was unceremoniously bundled out by Sanjay Gandhi and his cronies. In an interesting chapter in his book, he has vividly described how corruption, mismanagement and constant political and bureaucratic interference eroded the autonomy of Air India and hastened its decline. Even now, according to him, Air India has some best technical and non-technical staff but it lacks leadership. In 1972, he received the Padma Shri Award.

Das played a key role in strengthening and galvanizing the Association of Retired Senior IPS Officers (ARSIPSO). When the President of ARSIPSO, A.K. Dave, another stalwart of the Indian Police, suddenly died, Das stepped into his shoes as the President. I was a member of the Executive Committee and got the opportunity to know and frequently interact with him. Das in his early eighties was the seniormost member of our group but was most proactive and dynamic in his thoughts and outlook. He sincerely felt that retired officers of the Indian Police Service who, in their respective service careers, held high offices with distinction in different capacities, constituted a pool of unmatched expertise in spheres of law enforcement, national security and intelligence, and it would be a crowning pity if they hang up their boots, and become whiners, living in the world of yesterday and fail to use their knowledge and expertise. At a time, when the country faces security threats of the gravest magnitude, they cannot afford to be lotus eaters. They should constitute a think tank and step forward to help the government and society with well-thought-out and practical ideas and insights. He often quoted the example of the Indian Diplomats Association where the retired groups of Indian Foreign Service officers study and examine in depth various issues relating to external affairs and provide useful inputs to the government.

In his book *Memoirs of a Diplomat* he described his association with ARSIPSO as "resurrection", and observed aptly and perceptively, "I felt fulfilled as a former IPS officer. I realized how satisfying it was to belong to a service which plays a key role in the emerging new India. I also realized that I could understand the sensitivities and nuances in their role only because I took a long wandering route, very exciting, and full of new experiences."

B.S. Das always remained a gentleman to his fingertips and

generous to a fault. He was unfailingly gracious and had a knack of putting people at ease with his disarming candour. These shining qualities of head and heart endeared him to everyone with whom he worked and earned plaudits from many quarters.

He typified Swami Vivekananda's maxim, "Better wear out than rust out." I, along with a few members of ARSIPSO, met him over lunch at the India International Centre about a month before his death. He talked animatedly about current affairs, and also of further measures to galvanize ARSIPSO, and streamline its functioning. Little did we know that death was beckoning him, and he was soon going to leave us forever.

Towards me, he had been always very kind, indulgent and appreciative. In an illuminating foreword for my book *Terrorism Around the World*, he very perceptively observed, "The word terrorism indicates terror, cruelty and conscious destruction of the unarmed innocents. No religious philosophy supports this. Most of those killed are unarmed civilians, women and children, and, by their co-religionists."

His accomplished wife, Nirmala Das, had been a source of great strength and inspiration, and her death was a grievous loss to him. The personal tragedy saddened and subdued him but did not douse his zest for life. He remained positive, alert and full of beans, and a picture of grace and poise, and exuded a benign charm till his last breath. He constantly exhorted ARSIPSO members to make it a more vibrant and dynamic organization. I wish ARSIPSO cherishes his dream, and feels inspired and rejuvenated. His vision and zest for life was transformative. I salute the deathless memory of this indomitable police officer. He had the vision of catalyzing the matchless expertise of senior police officers for strengthening the sinews of national security and inspiring others to imbibe the same outlook. His abiding legacies have to be cherished and sustained.

12

R. Rajgopal: A Charismatic Leader

Chaman Lal

DG BSF Rustamji used to address Mr. Rajgopal as Raj, and treat him with the affection a teacher feels for his brightest pupil. Though much younger in age and length of service, Mr. Rustamji recognized his competence and maturity and would invariably consult him on important matters within and beyond his charge as IG (Intelligence) BSF.

Mr. Rajgopal was the senior-most member of the small group of IPS officers. Mr. Rustamji, while he was serving as IGP, Madhya Pradesh, was chosen to raise the Border Security Force (BSF). Rustamji took Mr. Rajgopal with him to Delhi in December 1965. He had spotted the young colleague in the early 1950s in Nagpur during his days as PM Jawaharlal Nehru's Security Officer. Once as the PM was being driven to the Governor's House with Mr. Rustamji sitting beside him in the car and the Governor's ADC Rajgopal sitting with the driver on the front seat, a cycle rickshaw puller with a knife in his hand, made a sudden dash towards Nehru. Rajgopal, in a rare show of bold alertness, jumped out of the car and caught the man and aborted the attempted assassination. For this act of courage, valour and dedication to duty at great risk to his own life, Mr. Rajgopal was awarded the President's Police Medal for Gallantry in the infancy of his career.

The son of a Professor of Philosophy in Government College, Nagpur, Rajgopal was one among eleven siblings—four boys and seven girls. He taught History for two years before joining in 1948, belonging to the first batch of the Indian Police Service (IPS) instituted to replace the Imperial Police (IP) of the British time. He started his career in the Central Province and Brar (CP and Brar) and was allotted to the MP Cadre when the new state was formed in November 1956.

I take great pride in belonging to the Cadre (MP) of Mr. Rustamji and Mr. Rajgopal, I cherish my closeness with both during their service careers and also after retirement. Both had left MP a year before I joined as ASP Bhopal in December 1966 on completion of my training at Mount Abu. Everyone in the MP Police seemed to be missing Mr. Rustamji, the most adorable and revered figure. He became the head of the Force (IGP) at the young age of 42 and led the MP Police for seven years (1958-65) with rare distinction earning a great reputation for his progressive outlook, welfare mindedness and a unique sense of fairness in everything, big or small in professional as well as personal matters.

Mr. Rajgopal had left behind only a few but ardent admirers who would often refer to his intimate knowledge of Police Regulations and Procedures and mastery in investigative skills. As the District SP and later as Range DIG, he was known to give utmost attention to the working of Police Station. He was remembered by many for the thoroughness of his inspection notes and quality of supervisory memos and case scrutinies. It was a treat for the young new entrants to the service to read the reports and notes penned by Mr. Rajgopal. However, there were a few detractors also among his peers who felt uncomfortable with all-round praise for his professional competence and impeccable integrity. Some would go to the extent of accusing him of some kind of moral terrorism by his totally uncompromising approach in the matter of professional probity and personal cleanliness. As I had no occasion to serve directly under him in MP, I could not judge the fairness or otherwise of this criticism. However, later while serving directly under him in the Shah Commission of Inquiry, I observed closely his insistence on professional thoroughness with utmost concern for integrity but without any undue inflexibility and imposition of his norms and standards on others.

Mr. Rajgopal spent nearly 10 years in the BSF as DIG and later as IG (Intelligence) and established the Intelligence Wing on modern lines, creating a wide network of sources, introducing sophisticated scientific equipment and special devices for intelligence collection. The contribution of the Intelligence Wing to the spectacular achievements of the young force in the 1971 Indo-Pak War and liberation war of Bangladesh was duly recognized by awarding the DIG (Intelligence) Rajgopal, the national award of Padmashri.

Since Mr. Rajgopal had left MP on deputation to the BSF before earning his promotion as IGP, his experience in the State Police remained confined to functional (SP) and supervisory (DIG) level with no opportunities to display the leadership qualities associated with directional (IGP or head of the force) level. This gap was adequately filled when he was promoted and posted as IGP Delhi in 1974. He took the new challenge of policing the country's capital with great enthusiasm duly blessed by his mentor Mr. Rustamji, who was instrumental in getting him this posting. Mr. Rajgopal stayed just one year in this post and was forced to leave under unfortunate circumstances, paying the price of his scrupulous adherence to professional duties and ethical norms. However, he found it to be the most satisfying professional experience of his career.

Shri P.S. Bawa, my batch mate from the UT cadre tells me that Mr. Rajgopal was the first head of force the Delhi Police had, who gave maximum attention to bringing about improvements in the Police Station working and Police-Public relations in India's capital city. He made it a part of his daily routine to visit one Police Station and spend an hour or so to review the progress of ongoing cases and give specific directions to the SHO. Equipped with professional excellence and integrity of the highest order, Mr. Rajgopal enjoyed a high moral position and was heard with respect and taken seriously by everyone.

He is remembered by many in the rank and file for a small but significant matter of his tenure as IGP Delhi, concerning the scale of winter clothing for Delhi Police personnel. A much needed but long neglected item of winter clothing, an overcoat, for protection against the extreme cold of Delhi winter was introduced at the personnel instance of the outsider IGP.

The MP Police in Mr. Rustamji's time was considered the pioneer in the matter of welfare schemes for education, healthcare and livelihood issues of police families. Mr. Rajgopal got some of these replicated in the Delhi Police by bringing on deputation, a distinguished police officer, viz. Yusuf Rahim from MP Police as DIG (Adm). Another outstanding police officer of MP, Ashok Patel, known for his legendary investigative skills, was also inducted to promote excellence in crime detection work. The bank van robbery case and the Vidya Jain murder case of 1974 were the landmark achievements of the Delhi Police during Mr. Rajgopal's tenure.

Mr. Rajgopal is also credited with firm, fair and effective police handling of the infamous Sadar Bazaar riots of 1974. In an extraordinary display of courage, valour and dedication to duty he personally led the police contingent together with DIG Ved Marwah into one of the worst-affected pockets of the communal conflagration and freed it from the total control of rioters. For this outstanding act of bravery, Mr. Rajgopal was awarded the Bar to the President's Police Medal for Gallantry, that he had earned years ago in Nagpur.

Mr. Rajgopal's term as IGP Delhi ended suddenly, though not unexpectedly for him. He sensed it coming because of his principled stance in a criminal case involving a top industrialist close to Sanjay Gandhi. His premature removal from Delhi had the effect of denying him the President's Police Medal for Distinguished Service in his turn which was granted a year later after the Emergency was lifted.

The high point of Mr. Rajgopal's career was his appointment as Secretary, Shah Commission of Enquiry (referred to as Commission hereafter) to enquire into Emergency excesses constituted by the Janata Government in June 1977 under the chairmanship of Justice J.C. Shah, a retired Chief Justice of India. His selection for the job was a clear recognition of his professional standing and proven ability to stand up and speak the truth to the powers-that-be. He took up the new job on June 17, 1977 and made the Commission fully functional in less than two months. Armed with full powers from the Chairman to select the teams of investigators, he visited a number of states and brought on deputation police officers and administrative officers of extraordinary calibre and high integrity such as B.K. Panigrahi and Sankar Sen (Odisha), S.K. Sharma (Rajasthan), R.C. Sharma (Haryana), H.D. Rao (UP), R.C. Jha (MP), R.S. Rathore (Income Tax Department), etc.

I had completed just seven months as SP Shivpuri (MP) on return from nine years in the BSF. I received the orders to join the Commission, in relaxation of the two-year cooling-off rule. I joined the Commission as OSD in September 1977, and was jointly with P.S. Mehta, an IAS officer of Gujarat, assigned the sensitive subject of the abuse of MISA detention powers in various states during the period of emergency.

This was the first time that I worked directly under Mr. Rajgopal. Because of my closeness to him developed during nine years in the BSF, I had the advantage of watching him from close quarters; it was like witnessing a human dynamo in action. He used to work for 12-14 hours a day and spend a big chunk of Sundays and holidays also in the office. Reviewing the work of individual investigation teams, comprising a DIG and two-three SPs, was an essential part of his daily routine. Besides examining the progress of investigation, he would, as a matter of sacred obligation, emphasize to us two major concerns of the Chairman Justice Shah. One, we should strictly observe the professional norms of fairness and objectivity and never let ourselves be used for any political purpose. Second, protecting the utter purity and integrity of the Commission's proceedings. This must be an article of faith for every member of the staff. He would remind us repeatedly that as the Commission's investigators, our job was to gather facts, all facts, including those which might go in favour of the accused person so as to arrive at the truth of the allegations made by the complainant. There was no review meeting wherein Mr. Rajgopal would not emphasize the importance of purity of investigation and the mandate to keep all our actions lawful and our conduct ethical.

The Commission made a quick start with as many as 50,000 complaints received till July 31, 1977, notified as the last date of submission of complaints. The public hearings started from September 29, 1977, and concluded on July 7, 1978.

The emergency case—the declaration of emergency and the chain of circumstances leading to it—was not part of any complaints referred to, or received by the Commission. It was the Commission's decision, taken at the level of the Chairman and the Secretary, that the full account of circumstances leading to the declaration of emergency by the President of India, on the recommendations of PM Indira Gandhi, without the mandatory constitutional provision of consultation with the cabinet, should be made public.

Mr. Rajgopal's dynamic personality and transparent style of working imparted an intellectual aura to the court-like atmosphere at Patiala House, the seat of the Commission. Mr. Rajgopal used to hold regular interactions on various public issues of the Commission's interest with top journalists such as B.G. Verghese, Nikhil Chakraborty, Kuldip Nayar, Nihal Singh and Romesh Thapar. Well-known intellectuals and academicians, such as Rajni Kothari, K.N. Raj and Jaydev Sethi, were special invitees for consultation on various issues. The most frequent visitor to the Secretary's room was Arun Shourie, whose involvement brought the Commission great appreciation from the UK media. Bernard Levin of the *London Times* wrote a series of articles on Delhi detention cases based on the materials from the Commission's proceedings sent by Arun Shourie.

On the Hearing Days, the Commission's court room used to be

packed well above capacity with enthusiastic people from various walks of life, retired bureaucrats, lawyers, rights activists and media personnel of both sexes. They relished the powerful figures of emergency—R.K. Dhawan, Navin Chawla, Jagmohan, S. Tamta and P.S. Bhinder, et al, cowering uncomfortably under the stern but gentle questioning by Justice Shah.

The Shah Commission of Inquiry was perhaps the only Commission which completed its assigned work in a period of just 15 months without asking for any extension. It presented two interim reports, first on March 11, 1978 and the second on April 26, 1978, before submitting the third and final report on August 6, 1978. It had finished all inquiries and administrative work and was prepared to close down on September 30, 1978 as originally scheduled. However, its formal term had to be extended up to December 31, 1978 for technical reasons in order to give legal cover to the various state authorities and the reports emanating from them on the complaints marked to them by the Commission.

At the farewell lunch hosted to Chief Justice Shah by the Commission staff, the grand old man, not given to any emotional ties, offered his Sheaffer pen and Parker ball point pen to Mr. Rajgopal, and said, "I have used these for some time, I would like you to keep them with you." Mr. Rajgopal was deeply moved, and considered the gift more than a compensation for indignity, as we soon learnt, he was going through at the hands of the top bureaucrats in the matter of his next posting.

Converting his last address to the Commission staff on August 7, 1978 into some kind of a valedictory address, Mr. Rajgopal said, "If it were given to anyone to choose his moment of death, I would choose it to be today only, if for the reason that I could look my master in the face, and tell him that I have done what I was expected to do, and, as well as, I possibly could."

Mr. Rajgopal refused the government offer of the post of Secretary, SC/ST Commission, telling the Union Home Secretary, that after serving in the Shah Commission of Inquiry, that was the summit of all Commissions, he had no desire to work in any other Commission. The Chief Minister MP, V.K. Saklecha, offered him the post of the State IGP, but he declined, saying that, as he had missed getting it in 1974, on political considerations, he did not want it then after two officers junior to him had held it.

The government, particularly, the Home Secretary seemed determined not to offer him a regular post of the Secretary in a Union Ministry, the exclusive domain of the IAS.

Although everybody in the government including, the Cabinet Secretary and the Home Secretary praised the Commission's reports in glowing terms and openly attributed it to Mr. Rajgopal's personal touch in everything, particularly, their superb drafting, they were unwilling to accept his claim for the Secretary's post. We all felt sorry for him seeing him turning bitter and frustrated after 18 months of remarkable work as the Commission's Secretary. I distinctly recall that it was during this period that he had, while in conversation with a select group of the Commission's DIG/SP, said something that struck me as very profound and painful. "From now onwards I will be leading a posthumous existence with the best part of my life left behind."

Mr. Rajgopal took it as his personal responsibility to ensure that all officers, who had joined the Commission on deputation, were suitably relocated in the central government organizations even if it required relaxation of the deputation rules. He saw to it that none of them suffered any financial loss or any other form of humiliation for having opted to serve in the Commission under his persuasion. He had to make a number of visits to the Home Secretary for this at the cost of his dignity and self-respect.

In January 1978, Mr. Rajgopal was posted as DG Bureau of Police Research and Development (BPR&D) in the pay scale of Rs. 3,250. It was his decision not to ask for admissible protection of his pay (Rs. 3,500) as personal to him, simply because he did not want to cause hurt or embarrassment to two of his senior colleagues, Mr. C.V. Narasimhan, Director CBI and Ashwini Kumar, DG BSF who were serving in the Rs. 3,250 scale.

Mr. Rajgopal soon moved from BPR&D to CRPF after the latter was rocked by police strike in some pockets of the force, and the incumbent DG had to be removed to make way for a more energetic and effective leadership. He took up the new challenge enthusiastically and started visiting all the units, particularly, the far flung ones and succeeded in restoring order and discipline in the force in a few weeks.

Indira Gandhi returned to power in 1980, following the defeat of the Janata Party Government in the mid-term elections. The prominent faces of the emergency who were indicted by the Commission and were required to be prosecuted were back in positions of power. Harassment of those, who had served in the Commission started. Mr. Rajgopal was the first to be hit, and was repatriated with immediate effect to his parent cadre MP. Instead of returning to MP, and getting some insignificant post in the charged political environment, Mr. Rajgopal chose to take premature retirement, about ten months before his normal superannuation, that was due in December 1980. He vacated the government accommodation within the permissible period of two months, and moved to a small rented house, arranged with great efforts, by two of his loyal subordinates.

It did not take Mr. Rajgopal long to reconcile with the new situation, and regain peace with himself. He started living as a good Samaritan, helping his old retired subordinates of BSF, Delhi Police and CRPF, in their service problems, particularly pension matters. He would travel by ordinary DTC buses to visit the various offices to plead their cases.

Mr. Rajgopal suffered brain haemorrhage on January 24, 1990 while deboarding a bus. It was diagnosed at the AIIM, New Delhi, as a case of brain tumour, beyond the scope of surgery. He underwent a few sessions of chemotherapy, followed by physiotherapy, but died on May 16, 1990. I was at that time, posted as IGP (Telecom), MP, Bhopal. I used to travel by night train to be with him on every Saturday morning, and stay till Sunday evening, to catch the return train to Bhopal. Before leaving, I would ask him whether he would like me to come on the following Saturday. I can still see before my mind's eye his sickly, but calm face, and his barely audible soft whisper, "Yes, of course!"

Mr. Rajgopal was a deeply religious man, who would invariably visit the three famous shrines—Tirupathi, Padmanabha and Guruvayoor—before starting any important undertaking, professional, or personal, and also by way of thanksgiving, on its completion. He had an unshakable faith in the blessings and protection of the supreme power, and would attribute all his successes and achievements to the divine will.

Mr. Rajgopal was not a socialite, or a 'party' man, and did not believe in cultivating contacts, but liked inviting his colleagues and friends, in small groups of 7-8 persons, to private dinners at his place, occasionally. The guests used to enjoy the simple vegetarian South Indian food, cooked by Mrs. Rajgopal. Those were the rare moments when one could see the serious-minded workaholic, open and relaxed, chatting cheerfully, and making witty remarks.

Mr. Rajgopal sought ordinariness in everything—his choice of food, clothes, means of entertainment, and normal joys of life. This insistence on simplicity practised with stubborn sincerity, made Mr. Rajgopal one of the most extraordinary policemen of our time.

13

B.K. Roy: A Forgotten Police Chief

B.P. Saha

My long stint in the police service has given me the opportunity to work under several stalwarts such as K.F. Rustamji, D. Sen, John Lobo, R.D. Singh, B.B. Mishra, G.B. Majumdar, and several others, who made a deep impression on me. Their sterling leadership qualities and pragmatic steps taken by them for refurbishing the police image, place them on a high pedestal. Besides, these outstanding personalities, there are many police officers whose meaningful contributions to professionalize the police and improving its image, remain unknown, unnoticed and unsung. I shall mention one such dynamic police personality, Shri B.K. Roy, whose relentless endeavour to bridge the gap between the police and the people, and improve police functioning, remained unknown and unnoticed.

I recollect that at the fag end of 1964, preparations for the passing out parade of the 16th batch of the IPC probationers in the Central Police Training College, Mt. Abu, Rajasthan, were afoot. On the eve of the passing-out ceremony, senior police officers from different states are invited to participate in a seminar, as well as to attend the passing-out ceremony. I came to know that B.K. Roy, a DIG from Orissa State, had arrived as one of the invitees for the seminar. I was allotted the Orissa cadre, and was, therefore, eager to meet him and know from him about the Orissa police. However, I was unable to meet him due to the busy schedule of the ceremony. Fortunately, one afternoon, I noticed him along with a few senior officers, walking by the side of the Nakki Lake in Mt. Abu. Mustering courage, I introduced myself to Mr. Roy and others accompanying him. Indeed, his response was very warm and positive. He asked a few questions regarding my education, family as well as reasons for choosing the police career.

His personality, bearing, frankness and eagerness for conversation with a beginner in the police impressed me. I was asked to join the boat riding, which was a pleasant experience. A senior officer questioned me if I knew how to row and swim. Mr. Roy intervened and stated that persons from East Bengal (now Bangladesh) often have to live in waterlogged areas, surrounded by rivers and canals and water pools. Heavy rains and floods, very often disrupt their normal life. In rural areas, country boats are the common means of communication. Saha hailing from that part of the country must have been good in rowing. Later on, I demonstrated my skill for a few minutes. Mr. Roy carried an expensive still camera and used it frequently.

At the seminar, he placed his points of view firmly and countered opponents' arguments analytically. In fact, he made a profound impression on the minds of the distinguished participants. I was delighted to watch a forceful personality and an able leader of the police. I was inclined to believe that breaking away from the past legacy of the police, many dynamic police officers will project the police in the right perspective and inspire the rank and file to serve the people intelligently, diligently and with a missionary zeal.

After joining the Orissa cadre in January 1965, I learnt that B.K. Roy belonged to the first batch of 1948. He was the son of a senior judicial service officer and had studied in Patna, and stayed in the university and college hostels. He was a gourmet, relished good food, and was keen to entertain class friends. His hostel friends, in recognition of his love for food, used to fondly call him, "Bhojan Krishna Roy."

He was DIG of the Southern Range, Berhampur, comprising Ganjam, Koraput, Kalahandi and Phulbani districts. His reputation as Range DIG was a matchless impetus for idealistic young officers, wanting to refurbish the police image. But it was also known that he was a hard taskmaster and a strict disciplinarian, conversant with police rules and procedure, and unsparing for ease-loving subordinates. His inspection notes were exhaustive, instructive and carried the stamp of professionalism. He was upright and would support the right cause and protect the subordinates, when they were right.

As Additional District SP of Koraput, I had the opportunity to work under him. Truly, his visits to the Districts was an alarm bell to clear the pending matters, including investigations, accounts, training, etc. I had immensely benefited from his guidance on investigation of special report cases (SR cases) and prompt finalization of quasi-judicial departmental proceedings. In short, his courage and capability to take a firm stand in critical situations deeply inspired many of us. A few examples of his extraordinary courage of conviction are still fresh in my mind.

Once he was camping with his wife in Koraput. He arranged a lunch in the Circuit House and invited all the gazetted police officers along with their wives. Needless to say, such a gesture was heart-warming and enthused the subordinate staff.

In district administration, often the rift between the District Magistrate and the Superintendent of Police generates an uneasy ambience. In a particular case, both were direct recruits and good friends before joining the district. Then they fell out. In fact, the ego and personal vanity of the District Magistrate muddied the water. Sadly, their friendship ended in acrimony. The DM tried to find fault in police operations on any pretext. Finally, it reached its climax when the DM recorded adversely in SP's Annual Confidential Report (ACR). The ACR with DM's observations was sent to the higher authorities. As Range DIG, B.K. Roy disagreed with DM's remarks, and pointed out that the remarks were erroneous and biased. DIG's views were accepted by the higher authorities and the DM's adverse comments were expunged. In short, relying on experience, I can vouch that very few senior officers will take up cudgels for junior colleagues in this fashion.

Another incident to protect an officer from the wrath of the Chief Minister is noteworthy. Indeed, it is a message for the top brass to learn how a biased move towards victimization of an officer for alleged failure in discharging duties fairly and diligently, was neutralized. The annual car festival in the sea beach town Puri, Orissa, is celebrated with utmost devotion and solemnity. Ten to twelve lakh pilgrims, emotionally-surcharged, assemble every year to pull the chariots of Lord Jagannath, his brother Balabhadra and sister Subhadra. Devotees believe that if they can touch the rope and pull it, salvation of the soul in future is ensured. Faith is paramount, defying logic and prudence. Thousands of policemen are deployed to control the zealous devotees and crowd, maintain law and order, traffic, avert accidents and assist in dragging the chariots. Following the practice, DM, SP and SDO remain in charge of each chariot, separately, and responsible to ensure its smooth pulling, without any hindrance.

On the fateful day, unfortunately, the chariot under the SP's charge, while moving, hit a street lamppost. One of its wheels was badly damaged and it lost its capacity to proceed. It needed a major repair and, therefore, had to be stranded right at the spot, with the deity placed on the chariot. In fact, breakdown of a chariot, and its unceremonious halt is considered to be a bad and inauspicious omen. Crowds gathered and the townsmen were frightened, anticipating an ugly calamity, including an epidemic, pestilence, countless deaths, etc. The panic-stricken people cried for an early solution for averting the impending disaster. Religious devotees and orthodox people, sentimentally upset, were up in arms to denounce and penalize the police. The CM was present in the town to witness the festival. IGP (B.K. Roy) was present on the spot, watching the police's performance under the SP. The CM was under tremendous pressure from the conservative and orthodox elements to take some immediate action against the police. Hence, he was trying to find a scapegoat, and thereby pacify the emotionally surcharged people. He called the IGP and said that the police's failure was the root cause of the terrible mishap. Finally, he said that he was going to suspend the Superintendent of Police.

IGP vehemently argued and defended the police and the SP's role. Being present at the spot, he directly watched the execution of the police and SP's supervision. He pleaded that thousands of devotees drag the chariots, inspired by religious spirit and zeal. Crowds often go berserk and pull the rope recklessly. It has no brake and, therefore, difficult to control speed. The road is not sufficiently spacious to accommodate three chariots to move together through the mass of crowd. More than adequate cops had been deployed under the SP's supervision but were handicapped before the countless devotees, desperate to touch and pull the rope.

However, the CM was adamant to punish the SP. Failing to convince the CM, the IGP firmly told the CM that since he was present on the spot and involved with the entire episode, the responsibility of the mishap should be placed upon him. The government should, therefore, suspend the IGP instead of the SP. The CM was taken aback. He could never imagine the IGP's firm stand to sacrifice his career for the sake of the SP. Fortunately, the CM was a seasoned administrator, who knew how to value the morale of the police force. He kept the action in abeyance, and eventually dropped the idea. Indeed, such a selfless and fearless stand to support a just cause and protect a junior colleague, ignoring self-interest, has been seldom witnessed in the annals of the Indian police.

Regrettably, a few officers were not comfortable with the IGP's call for toning up the police. They secretly instigated the disgruntled elements to question the IGP's wisdom. He got the wind of it and deputed a few senior officers known for their integrity to open a dialogue with them and redress their grievances. He thought the cloud had blown over. Hence, he made a holiday plan for a few days and left Cuttack, failing to judge the extent of the simmering discontent. In his absence, the agitation gained momentum. On receiving information midway, he discontinued the journey and returned to the police headquarters. Meanwhile, a group of subordinates gathered and virtually surrounded his bungalow, shouting slogans. Some senior officers stood by his side, interacting with the angry cops. Soon, the situation was brought under control. But the IGP's image was considerably dented. Criticism piled upon criticism. Members of the Legislative Assembly demanded his removal from the post. Many impartial persons also joined the chorus, and argued that the leadership of the police should be given to a new hand.

The meeting with the Chief Minister was far from cordial. The CM sarcastically stated that the IGP allowed the unrest to grow and thereafter proceeded on leave. It was tantamount to shirking responsibility. IGP refuted CM's statement and asserted that if the CM could cite an iota of evidence that the IGP directly, or indirectly provoked the agitation, or instigated the unruly elements, he would tender his resignation, at once. The CM was again at a loss. However, he did not wish to stretch the conversation further.

Thereafter, the government unceremoniously removed him from the post of IGP and assigned him an inconspicuous posting. Later on, he went on deputation as the Director of Sardar Vallabhbhai Patel National Police Academy and he retired from there. He won accolades as a successful Director of NPA.

Roy's abiding legacy to the police fraternity, and particularly to the members of the Indian Police Service, is his unmatched professional expertise and courage to take bold decisions, without caring for personal interests. At a time when expediency is the keyword for many in the service, he stood aloof and apart as an officer of high integrity and had the courage of convictions. A stern disciplinarian, he was, at times, very harsh and inflexible, but always kept in view the interests of the service. This, at times, made him unpopular with the politicians and some of his subordinates, but out of the maelstrom of controversy and criticism, he emerged as an upright and courageous officer and a superb police professional. He left his footprints and made an impact wherever he worked.

14

K.P.S. Gill: A Lion-Hearted Police Chief!

D.N.S. Shrivastava

On joining the Assam Police in 1965, I met K.P.S. Gill quite a few times at police functions. But my first meaningful interaction with him took place in Calcutta in 1977, during the conference of SSP of Naxal-affected districts of Eastern States of India. We stayed together in the Assam House, Calcutta, for a few days. My first impression of him was that he was a knowledgeable person. His approach to policing was unconventional. He often recited Urdu and English poetry in the course of conversation.

He was born on December 29, 1934 at Lahore. He was a postgraduate in English literature and belonged to the 1957 batch of the IPS. He was seven years senior to me in service and five years in age. During his tenure in Assam, I had the privilege of working with him as SP and later as DIGP Range for about six years. I came in close touch with him during these years.

On joining the Indian Police Service, Mr. Gill was allotted to the Assam cadre where, from 1958 to 1983, he handled with notable success, a range of difficult assignments including law and order management during periods of extended political strife and the emergence of terrorism in the state. His various assignments during this tenure included: Containment of mass political demonstrations and violence, counter-terrorism, protection of critical infrastructure, including major oil-installations and pipelines, direction of armed police and para-military units and law and order management.

On deputation to the Government of India, he served as a senior officer in the Border Security Force in the State of Jammu & Kashmir where containment of infiltration and cross-border terrorism sourced in Pakistan were his crucial responsibilities.

He also served with great distinction as a senior officer in the Central Industrial Security Force, with responsibilities that covered security of critical infrastructure, major industries, major ports and oil installations. Despite initial opposition from the nuclear establishment, he trained and inducted CISF cadres into the security and protection of nuclear installations in the country.

He served as the Director General of the Central Reserve Police Force—a unique national armed police force that handles a range of critical internal security challenges, including terrorism, rioting and other patterns of mass political violence. He headed the Committee for the creation of a new special response force for situations of communal violence and other patterns of mass civil violence: the Rapid Action Force (RAF).

Mr. Gill led the successful campaign against fundamentalist and international cross-border terrorism in the Indian State of Punjab. As the Director General of Police, Punjab, he led a complex succession of multi-Force counter-terrorism operations that involved the Armed Police, para-Military and Military units that fought and neutralized terrorism after Jihadi terrorism in Punjab emerged as the most serious threat to national integrity in the 1980s. He was specially inducted into the state as Inspector General of Police [Operations] and later elevated to the rank of Additional Director General of Police, and eventually Director General of Police [DGP]. Within days of taking over as DGP, he mounted 'Operation Black Thunder', a critical success in the war against terrorism. A classical siege operation, Black Thunder was mounted against heavily armed and fortified terrorists in the holiest of Sikh shrines, the Golden Temple at Amritsar, and secured their surrender with minimal bloodshed. In two tenures as DGP Punjab [May 1988–December 1990 and November 1991–December 1995], he led one of the most successful and innovative counter-terrorist operations in the history of world terrorism, bringing Punjab back from the verge of disintegration to complete normalcy. This campaign was marked by radical strategic innovations and made revolutionary departures from conventional counter-terrorist theory that accorded primacy to the army in situations of escalating terror. It was the Punjab Police that spearheaded operations in the state and in the rest of India, including major metropolitan cities of Bombay, Calcutta, Pune and in the states of Uttar Pradesh, Assam, West Bengal, Maharashtra and Jammu & Kashmir. In some of these states, the Punjab Police personnel were deputed in strength for extended periods of time to assist the local authorities in putting an end to this international cross-border terrorism, that was being mounted from bases in Pakistan, and that was heavily supported by the Pakistani state.

During his Punjab tenure, he resolved two major hijacking crises involving terrorists taking control of civilian passenger aircraft and flying them into the Amritsar airport. Existing anti-hijack response procedures in the state were radically reviewed and revised under his direction to prevent the recurrence of such incidents. Tall, ramrod straight and taciturn, he knew the art of electrifying men under his charge. Before his embattled officers, he was the symbol of courage and defiance.

After his retirement from the Indian Police Service in December 1995, he held the following positions; he was the President,

Institute for Conflict Management, which he set up in 1997. He was also publisher and editor of the Institute's quarterly, *Faultlines, Writings on Conflict and Terrorism*, and publisher of the Institute's weekly newsletter, the *South Asia Intelligence Review*. As President of the Institute, he advised various governments, both in India and abroad, on issues relating to counter-terrorism and internal security, and had also provided expertise on security issues to various corporate entities. The Institute had executed major projects—including the world's largest open source website on terrorism and sub-conventional warfare in South Asia, the South Asia Terrorism Portal (www.satp.org).

He was the Security Advisor to the Chief Minister of Gujarat between May 2002–July 2002. He was specially appointed after the major Hindu-Muslim riots and killings in the state had persisted for over two months. He brought the situation under control within a week through a major reorganization of the Police Force and para-military deployment.

He was a Member of the North-East Study Group of the Ministry of Home Affairs.

He was a Member of the National Security Advisory Board [NSAB] constituted by the Government of India for the period December 1998–December 1999, to define the country's strategic perspectives and policy options on defence and internal security.

He was President, Indian Hockey Federation and Indian Hockey Confederation. He wrote regularly for a number of journals, newspapers and magazines on politics, economy, and governance, with a special focus on internal security and terrorism. He was also the author of *Knights of Falsehood* (1997), a book exploring both the abuse of the Sikh identity by politicians and terrorists in Punjab, and the teachings of the Sikh gurus.

He contributed frequently on subjects relating to terrorism and internal security, policing, politics, law and justice, in leading newspapers and magazines in India and delivered lectures at a number of premier academic and research institutions, including the National Defence College, the National Police Academy, the Indian Institute for Public Administration and various universities. He was awarded the Police Medal for Meritorious Services, 1972, President's Police Medal for Distinguished Service, 1982,

Padamshri, 1989 and also received a large number of honours from public and voluntary organizations for restoring normalcy in Punjab after over a decade of terrorism.

He died on May 26, 2017. I attended his funeral at Delhi. In death also he looked not dead but alive, about to speak. I saluted him and bade a final goodbye.

In my eyes, he will always remain an immortal and unconquerable, lion-hearted police chief who rendered great service to the country. He will always hold an abiding place of honour in the hearts of many all over the country.

15

J.N. Chaturvedi (1951 UP): An Unassuming Leader

K.K. Paul

To write about one of the most celebrated police officers of Delhi can be a daunting task. But as Sankar Sen asked me, it did not take me even a moment to decide that I must write about Jayendra Nath Chaturvedi, the first Police Commissioner of Delhi. I have had the good fortune of working with him and observing him at close quarters first as the Addl. SP of the South District of Delhi, and then as SP and DCP of the same district. My association with him continued even after he had left Delhi and joined the

Allahabad Railway Police. Subsequently, also, while he was the DGP of UP and Chairman of the UP Public Service Commission, we had occasions to meet during his visits to Delhi. Later, when I went to Dehradun as the Governor of Uttarakhand, I continued to pay my respects to him, till a few days before he was shifted from Max Hospital to Varanasi, where he died on March 12, 2019. At my last meeting, I was able to spend quite some time with Mrs. Saroj Chaturvedi in the hospital, but could not converse with him, and was only able to say a silent prayer at his bedside.

Every police officer is bound by the rules and the law, he is supposed to enforce, yet, while at the top, we find immense variation in the leadership styles. There have been charismatic leaders, like K.F. Rustamji and Ashwini Kumar, aggressive and strong leaders like Surender Nath and K.P.S. Gill, unassuming, but firm leaders like J.N. Chaturvedi and D. Sen. This is just a representative list, and with due respect to my seniors, who worked with some of them, it is entirely based on subjectivity. Ultimately, in police work, what matters is that the right leader should be at the right place, and at the right time. And, sometimes, as we are well aware, leaders emerge out of successful handling of certain very tight situations.

The world over there are numerous examples of various leadership styles, but very few of unassuming leaders. In the latter category, amongst the politicians, I would place Harry Truman of the USA, our own Lal Bahadur Shastri, and, amongst the police officers, J.N. Chaturvedi. A simple and an orthodox man, the strength and firmness of his mind took Mr. Chaturvedi to heights, to which very few officers may have risen. A unique quality of Mr. Chaturvedi, as a police officer, was never to have raised his voice, or become angry. Perhaps, this high level of patience and balance, came through his regular sessions of meditation and yoga.

After his superannuation, as the Chairman of the UP Public Service Commission, Mr. Chaturvedi decided to settle down at Dehradun, in view of its particularly salubrious climate. Dehradun, at that time, was a part of UP, as Uttarakhand came into being only in the year 2000. Yet, hardly any officer knew about him being in Dehradun. Despite his failing health, when he came to Raj Bhawan, to be present at my swearing in ceremony in January

2015, few people were with him. Only when I bent down to seek his blessings, did people recollect that here was, amongst them, the most unassuming Chairman of the UP Public Service Commission, and a celebrated DGP of the largest force of the country, and the first Police Commissioner of the national capital.

Though J.N. Chaturvedi rose to the highest position of the DGP in his own Uttar Pradesh cadre, and later became the Chairman of the UP Public Service Commission, it was as the first Commissioner of Delhi Police that he really earned his laurels as an inspirational, but an unassumimg leader. Joining Delhi Police at a most crucial time, when the morale of the force had suffered, and there was a crisis of leadership, he was, through his deft handling, able to restore a sense of professionalism, by setting a personal example. The post-emergency scenario had, perhaps, the maximum impact in Delhi, as a number of Delhi Police Officers had been hauled up by the Shah Commission, for the excesses. Besides, due to the naming game, played by some officers, there was an atmosphere of suspicion. Mr. Bhawanimal of the Rajasthan cadre (1950), who had taken over as the IGP of Delhi in December 1974, and had stayed on for the entire duration of emergency, had been replaced by M.C. Mishra of the MP cadre. He had come with a great reputation, but soon became a victim of intrigue, and was also shifted in just three months. It was in such a negative atmosphere, that Mr. Chaturvedi came to head the force in October 1977. His reputation, as a very hard taskmaster, a stickler for rules and impeccable integrity, had preceded him, and, in fact, there was already a speculation about postings and transfers. It was to the credit of Mr. Chaturvedi that, in his very first address, he was able to restore the confidence of officers to quite an extent.

Despite the IG of Delhi Police, being one of the senior-most officers in the country, and usually being handpicked by the Home Minister, the working equation with the Ministry, the Lt. Governor's establishment and Delhi Administration had always remained somewhat strained. Mr. Chaturvedi came to Delhi in October 1977, as IGP, and was soon faced with an atmosphere of intrigue, particularly in the post-emergency scenario, of complaints and counter-complaints. But, without any loss of time, he caught the bull by the horns, and arranged his priorities for the force.

There had been a serious agitation in Delhi Police in 1966, necessitating a Commission of Enquiry, which was chaired by Justice G.D. Khosla. The report submitted in 1968, in two volumes, had recommended extensive reorganization of the force and introduction of the Police Commissioner system. There was, however, a very strong lobby, which ensured delay in the implementation of the report, while, entirely, forgetting about the Commissioner of Police system. In the meantime, the new government had also constituted a Police Commission at the national level, chaired by Dharam Vira of the ICS. It is to the credit of Mr. Chaturvedi that, soon after his arrival in Delhi, he took up all these issues with the Home Minister Ch. Charan Singh, and things began to move in a positive direction. But after the initial thrust, despite the pressure of Ch. Charan Singh, who was known to be a supporter for the cause of police personnel, things again began to get stalled. People took advantage of the difference between the HM and the PM, and caused delays at every stage.

As the schism grew, Ch. Charan Singh resigned from the government. The Home portfolio was now directly looked after by the PM, later the MOS (Home), S.D. Patil, started looking after the day-to-day affairs, but the portfolio remained with the PM. One of the qualities of Mr. Chaturvedi was persistence for a good cause, and without waiting for a new HM to be appointed, he decided to bell the cat, and directly took up all the proposals with the Prime Minister. Morarji Desai was no green horn, as he had been the CM of the erstwhile Bombay state, and had also worked as a revenue officer. He was familiar with the Police Commissioner system of Bombay, Ahmedabad and Pune. At a meeting convened by the PM, clear directions were given to T.C.A. Srinivaswardhan, the powerful Union Home Secretary, to bring up a Bill for the Police Commissioner system in Delhi, at the earliest. After a month, Mr. Chaturvedi again sought an appointment with the PM on this very issue. Morarji Desai was at his administration's best, and the Union Home Secretary was at the receiving end. The PM would not listen to any excuse about delays, whether in the legal affairs departments, or the legislative wing, but reprimanded the Home Secretary, in no uncertain terms, and very clearly directed that now an ordinance, before the monsoon session of Parliament, should be brought in, for the Police Commissionerate.

The news spread like wild fire, and, lo and behold, within no time, the ordinance was approved by the cabinet, and the President also signed. For the first time in the country, thanks to Mr. Chaturvedi, a Police Commissionerate was established in Delhi on July 1, 1978, and that too through a Presidential Ordinance. The Delhi Police Act 1978 was passed by the Parliament, which received the Presidential assent in October 1978. But imagine, for the first three months, the Police Commissioner Delhi had to draw his powers from the Ordinance. It was a big feather in his cap, and a mission, which had been repeatedly stalled, had been accomplished. But now a bigger battle lay ahead. There were forces and important people, besides nay sayers, who wanted the Police Commissionerate to flounder, somehow.

As they say, there is never a dull moment in Delhi, and Mr. Chaturvedi had a significant exposure to an impending situation, within a few days of his arrival. On his very first full day in office, on October 3, 1977, the government had decided to arrest Indira Gandhi, in a case registered by the CBI. N.K. Singh, SP/CBI, was assigned this task, at a short notice, which explained the complete lack of preparation, coordination and attention to details, so essential for such an important and a sensitive matter. Y. Rajpal of the MP cadre, who had been earlier with the CBI, had joined Dehli Police as the Range DIG in the post-emergency reshuffles. He was coordinating with the CBI, but more on a personal note, rather than as DIG (R). The result was inadequate preparation on the ground for the possible fall-out on law and order, arising out of the arrest.

Any police officer could have anticipated this, but there appeared to be complete absence of coordination. The decision, that Mrs. Gandhi was being arrested, was perhaps conveyed to the Delhi Police only when N.K. Singh had reached 12 Willingdon Crescent, her residence. In the meantime, huge crowds began to gather outside her residence. In such matters, it is quite customary to have high level meetings in the MHA, but the distrust had reached such levels, that the plans were not shared even with the Chief Secretary, or the IGP Delhi, beforehand. The subsequent details of this case are all too well- known, and in public domain, as such, do not merit any reiteration, but suffice to say that our premier investigating agency, with this fiasco, had cut a very sorry figure, both at the national, as well as international levels.

As a strong section of the government was ab initio against such an exercise, and public criticism had begun to pile up, the MHA began to look for scapegoats. The poor policeman always finds himself at the receiving end in such matters. It was an ordeal by fire for Mr. Chaturvedi, as the prestige of the government had suffered, but he stood his ground, and ensured that the Delhi Police was completely insulated. Overnight, he became somewhat of a hero for the force. This case was also the beginning of the rift between Ch. Charan Singh and Morarji Desai coming out in the open.

With the morale of the police not very high, the post-emergency scenario had seen a spurt in crime. The 1977 figures of crime compared to 1976 went haywire, and seemingly there was a lot of pressure to undertake some course correction. Mr. Chaturvedi, however, stood firm for free registration. The situation improved considerably after the introduction of the Commissionerate in 1978, but the high crime rate in Delhi was being used as an issue against the Police Commissioner System. He stood firm on his stand for free registration, besides no use of third degree, but ultimately had to give way after the change of government in January, 1980. There was a new Home Minster, and he publicly professed at a meeting of Delhi Police Officers at FICCI auditorium that the police 'danda' had vanished, leading to lawlessness. He also wanted to change some District officers to set an example, but the Police Commissioner was quite firm in his address. Later, after a few days, when Mr. Chaturvedi had finished briefing the officers for the Republic Day arrangements, after the dress rehearsal, the government in a great hurry, issued orders reverting him back to his cadre. As such, for the R-Day function, virtually, at the last moment, there was a new Commissioner of Police, other than the one, who had made all the arrangements and overseen the dress rehearsal.

By giving instant recognition to good work, he was able to develop a cadre of inspired young police officers, who would later excel in their careers. In November 1978, during the Akali agitation, a small bunch of rowdies, brandishing naked swords, tried to disrupt the proceedings of the Nirankari Samagam, being held at India Gate Lawns. Kiran Bedi (1972), who was then posted as Addl. DCP of New Delhi Distt., somehow got isolated, yet, was able to single handedly deal with this armed bunch effectively. Mr. Chaturvedi, in no time, ensured that she was recognized by the government, who happily awarded a gallantry medal, laying the foundation of a great career.

A very strict disciplinarian, he ensured that youngsters remained within limits, and stayed away from the culture of partying and late nights, so prevalent in Delhi. On the other hand, he encouraged and organized dinner functions for officers, where, to the surprise of everyone, he, along with Mrs. Chaturvedi, always took the lead in singing a few melodies. He was also quite at home in singing shamans, as well as ghazals. A great family man, his qualities have been inherited by his two children, in ample measure. His son, Shashank Chaturvedi, is a world renowned scientist, currently posted as Director of the Institute of Plasma Research at Ahmedabad, and his daughter, Sucharita, a senior officer in PNB, has been happily married to an IPS officer.

When a warrant of detention had to be served on D. Sen, former Director of CBI, and he had to be escorted to Tihar Jail, I was given clear instructions that I should personally go to him, in uniform, and give him all the respect that is due to an officer of his seniority, and make him comfortable in my staff car.

His tenure in Delhi also saw one of the biggest law and order deployments ever. It was the Kisan rally of December 23, 1978, in which an estimated more than ten lakh people from the neighbouring states participated. Though it was seemingly a birthday celebration of Ch. Charan Singh, but, in reality, it was a show of strength in the ongoing tussle between him and the PM. In any such rally, the local police usually become over-occupied, with making Adm. arrangements for the outside forces. Mr. Chaturvedi had assigned very clear roles to each officer, and ensured compliance. As the Commissioner of Police, he was successful in getting maximum cooperation from the Delhi Government, civic agencies, as well as the Government of India. As several battalions of BSF had been deployed, Ashwini Kumar, DG/BSF, who was due to retire in a week's time, had certain issues, but then, it is known that Mr. Chaturvedi did not yield, as it was the CP/Delhi, who had to be in overall command.

The year 1979 saw police unrest, not only in the neighbouring states of Haryana and Punjab, but also amongst the ranks of some central forces. Headquarters of CISF and CRPF, being located in Delhi, the situation had to be handled with great tact and finesse. He was able to keep the Delhi Police completely insulated despite overwhelming numbers from these states in the force. On the other hand, the agitators of CISF and CRPF were handled very firmly. Whatever storms might have been brewing inside him, outwardly he was a picture of complete confidence, and an officer in total command and control of a situation, and this is what inspired all of us. His presence, alone, was sufficient to create an atmosphere of success.

A good man really cannot be kept down, and without waiting for long, he saw himself rising to be at the helm of affairs of the UP Police. By that time, the rank structure had also undergone a change, and the head of the force had become a DGP. A culture of encounters had crept in those days, but Mr. Chaturvedi was vehemently opposed to that. Though under great pressure from the then CM of UP, N.D. Tiwari, he was able to resist fake encounters, but only to an extent. Very soon, Shri Tiwari made him an offer, which he could not decline. He was to be the first ever IPS officer to be appointed as the Chairman of any State Public Service Commission. This was a great honour, indeed, for every police officer in the country. And as Field Marshall McArthur had said, old soldiers just fade away; this was perhaps an ideal fading away for a great policeman.

16

S. Venugopal Rao: A Policeman of Letters

Kamal Kumar

Law enforcement and academics are two disparate worlds, often considered poles apart from each other. Not so common, therefore, is to find a "man of letters" among law-enforcement professionals. Yet, in the personality of S. Venugopal Rao, one finds this rare blend so perfectly represented—a unique combination of a highly accomplished police officer on one hand and a passionate scholar, thinker, researcher and prolific writer on the other. His brilliant record as a thorough professional in his long career in kaleidoscopic assignments of the police organization, was matched or even surpassed by his significant contribution to the academics of policing and criminal justice. Not just that, his contribution to classical literature, in the form of satirical prose, poetry and plays, in English as well as Telugu has been equally magnificent.

Born on September 23, 1918 at Machilipatnam in Krishna district of Andhra Pradesh, Venugopal Rao had his early education at Machilipatnam, followed by Loyola College and Presidency College of Madras University, from where he obtained his Honours degree in Physics. He started his professional career initially with the Defence Accounts Service, and served as Deputy Controller of Defence Accounts at Meerut and Bombay. A few years later, when, with the exodus of British officers, post-independence, the Government of India launched a scheme of Special Recruitment Examination for the All India Services, he successfully competed in the same. Thus, he joined the Indian Police Service in 1949 (though assigned the seniority of 1946½, as per the extant policy, in consideration of his previous service in the Defence Accounts Department), and was allocated to the then Madras state.

In the early years of his police career, he served as Assistant Superintendent of Police at Peddapuram (East Godavari district) and Tenali (Guntur district), which were part of Madras state then. Post the creation of Andhra state, he had successful tenures as Superintendent of Police of Vizag North, Nellore and Guntur districts. After the merger of Andhra state with the Telugu-speaking region of Hyderabad state, he was handpicked for the coveted assignment of Deputy Commissioner of Police (Crimes) in Hyderabad City Police, followed by the post of Deputy Commissioner (Law & Order). He, thereafter, had a short stint as the Principal of the Police Training College of Andhra Pradesh at Anantapur, before being selected by the Intelligence Bureau, Government of India, especially to research and document a history of Indian Police, to mark its centenary. On return to the state, Venugopal Rao served the State Anti-Corruption Bureau as its Joint Director.

His long-lasting second innings with the central government were to begin soon after, when he joined the Central Bureau of Investigation in 1964 as the DIG steering the Research & Interpol Division of CBI. The posting offered him the stellar opportunity of representing India in numerous international conferences, including a quinquennial United Nations Congress on the

Prevention of Crime and the Treatment of Offenders[1]. After a few years in that job, he was promoted as the Joint Director in CBI, before he took over as the Director of the Institute of Criminology & Forensic Science (since rechristened as Lok Nayak Jayaprakash Narayan National Institute of Criminology & Forensic Science), in 1973. This institute indeed was his own brainchild. He finally took over as the Chief of the Bureau of Police Research & Development (BPR&D), the post from which he took voluntary retirement in 1976, to avail of the opportunity to join as a Senior Fellow at the Indian Institute of Advanced Study (IIAS) at Shimla, to pursue his academic interests—his first love. Shortly after that tenure, he was invited by the Indian Institute of Public Administration (IIPA), New Delhi, to establish a Department of Criminal Justice studies there, He, thereafter, worked with the Indian Council of Social Science Research (ICSSR) as a Senior Fellow. He finally hung his boots in 1988 and returned to Hyderabad with the intention to lead a retired life.

But that was not to be. Soon enough, his intense love for his profession and its academics spurred him on to establish a close association with the newly-created Andhra Pradesh Police Academy, still in its incipient stage. Here, he made an enormous contribution delivering lectures on a wide variety of themes and topics related to criminology, criminal justice administration, police science, and so on. In recognition of his sterling academic contribution to the Academy, the Government of Andhra Pradesh designated him as 'Professor Emeritus' of the Academy, duly issuing a Government Order (GO) in this regard.

Perhaps what can be termed as Venugopal Rao's most valuable contribution to the profession of Criminal Justice stemmed from his indefatigable efforts aimed at promoting the systematic study of criminology and forensic science in the country for the ultimate benefit of the criminal justice administration. These endeavours, *inter alia,* led to the establishment of the National Institute of Criminology & Forensic Science.

In fact, it had all started with a recommendation made by

1. He represented the country, for a second time, at the next Congress five years later, while posted as the Director of the Institute of Criminology & Forensic Science.

UNESCO, at a Symposium held at London in 1955, emphasizing the need for a systematic understanding of Criminology and Forensic Science among functionaries of the Criminal Justice Systems, and urging universities around the world to include these disciplines in their curricula. Even though UNESCO once again, in its Report in 1957, appealed to universities to introduce these subjects, and a subsequent Annual Conference of IGPs in India strongly endorsed this appeal, the response in the country was disheartening, with only the University of Sagar starting a Department of Criminology and Forensic Science in 1959[2]. This was obviously grossly inadequate for a country of India's size and its vast network of criminal justice system. The situation did not witness any improvement till the late 1960s.

Concerned over this, and even more about addressing the acute need for the training and education of in-service criminal justice functionaries in these subjects, Venugopal Rao, while working as a DIG in CBI, in March 1967, prepared a detailed Concept Note, elaborating the steps that needed to be taken to bring the subjects of Criminology and Forensic Science into the general stream of the university curricula "so that (i) the country's criminal justice system would in future get the required number of functionaries properly trained in those fields, and (ii) there would be a greater awareness and stimulation of thinking and research on the problems relating to crime and delinquency". He persuaded the Director CBI to send this Concept Note to the University Grants Commission (UGC). The UGC, thereupon, appointed a high-level Committee with Venugopal Rao also as a member.

The Committee, in turn, appointed a two-member Sub-Committee to go into the matter in detail, again with Venugopal Rao as one member. With the benefit of the experiences of universities and colleges of USA and other advanced countries running such courses that the formal and informal interactions of Venugopal Rao with them brought to bear upon the study, the Sub-Committee, after a detailed examination of various aspects, stressed in its report that it was necessary to provide positive encouragement to universities

---

2. Thanks to the Herculean effort made by the then IGP of Madhya Pradesh, K.F. Rustamji in persuading the University authorities and the state government.

in India to introduce courses of study in Criminology and Forensic Science. Apart from undergraduate degree programmes for fresh students, such universities should also start Diploma courses, mainly to cater to serving police and other criminal justice functionaries. For postgraduate courses and research in the two disciplines, it recommended the creation of an autonomous central institute, duly affiliated to a good university for the purpose of awarding degrees. The Sub-Committee also prepared a detailed blueprint for the proposed central institute. The main Committee of UGC strongly endorsed the Sub-Committee's report, including this blueprint.

After protracted correspondence on the subject between the UGC, the Ministry of Education and the Ministry of Home Affairs, the government finally decided to create the Institute under the aegis of the MHA. It was decided that, to begin with, the Institute should organize training programmes on different themes related to Criminology and Forensic Science for senior functionaries of all wings of the criminal justice system, pending its affiliation with a university for introducing postgraduate courses in the two disciplines for fresh students. Thus the 'Institute of Criminology & Forensic Science' came into existence in January 1972. The Institute, initially started under the umbrella of BPR&D, was soon accorded its own independent identity, with Venugopal Rao taking over as its first full-fledged Director in 1973. It was subsequently re-christened as the National Institute of Criminology & Forensic Science (NICFS). Later, as part of the commemoration of the birth centenary of Lok Nayak Jayaprakash Narayan, at the instance of the Ministry of Culture, the Institute was renamed as 'Lok Nayak Jayaprakash Narayan National Institute of Criminology and Forensic Science', vide Ministry of Home Affairs Resolution No. 10/4/2003-NICFS dated October 3, 2003.

The Institute has rendered yeoman service as perhaps the only institution providing joint training programmes for functionaries of all wings of the criminal justice administration, namely, the police, prosecution, judiciary, prisons and correctional services, as well as forensic science laboratories. Besides, officers of the civil administration, defence services, and customs department have also participated in some of its training programmes relevant to them. Since the Institute's inception, more than 35,000 senior officers have availed the benefit of these training courses. Research in subjects relating to Criminology and Forensic Science has also been an area of focus for the Institute, with numerous useful study projects and their findings to its credit. Under a scheme of doctoral fellowship offered by the Institute to promising students, it has produced numerous successful scholars who pursued their PhD research work under the guidance of the Institute's erudite faculty members. In the course of time, the Institute also started running postgraduate programmes—Master of Arts in Criminology and Master of Science in Forensic Science—under affiliation with the Guru Gobind Singh Indraprastha University, New Delhi—thus, ultimately effectuating the dream of Venugopal Rao in full.

In addition, scores of universities in the country—pushed by the UGC—have, in the subsequent years, introduced the subjects of Criminology and Forensic Science in their curricula, with many of them creating full-fledged departments of Criminology and Forensic Science. All thanks to Venugopal Rao's persuasive initiative in this regard.

This apart, Venugopal Rao also made an enormous contribution to academic literature on policing and criminal justice. He authored more than a dozen books and monographs on professional subjects of crime, criminality, and criminal justice, besides contributing numerous articles and papers in academic journals of repute from time to time. His masterpieces include *Facets of Crime in India* (Allied Publishers, 1963), *Power and Criminality* (Allied, 1976), *Dynamics of Crime: Spatial and Socio-Economic Aspects of Crime in India* (IIPA, New Delhi, 1981), *Crime in Our Society: A Political Perspective* (Vikas Publishing House, 1982), *Police Administration* (ed), (IIPA, New Delhi, 1982), *Human Rights and Criminal Justice* (Indian Law Institute, New Delhi, 1983), *Perspectives in Criminology* (ed), (IIAS, Shimla, 1985), *Crime, Law and the Citizen* (Indian Law Institute, New Delhi, 1986), *Victims of Crime* (Allied, 1989), *Criminal Justice: Problems and Perspectives in India* (Konark Publishers, 1991), *Elements of Modern Criminology* (AP Police Academy, 1992).

Special mention must be made of his classic work, *The Baton and The Pen—Four Decades with the Indian Police* (Konark, 1993), This book, documenting his memoirs, is described by Amazon on its website as a book that "deals with the changing texture of policing in India and the challenges of tomorrow that reads like a novel".

Besides enriching academic literature on serious subjects of policing and criminal justice, Venugopal Rao, a gifted writer, also contributed significantly to fiction, both in English and Telugu. His short stories in English were published in the reputed periodical *Illustrated Weekly of India,* over years. As a litterateur, he exhibited an uncanny ability to indulge in satire in English as well as in Telugu, and with equal felicity in both the languages. A highly popular book in Telugu that was authored by him, *Police Venkataswamy Kathalu,* is a collection of short stories encapsulating numerous policing episodes that capture in a humorous style the resourcefulness as well as foibles of police subordinates. The book has gone into many editions after its first publication in 1993 and is still in great demand. The royalty proceeds of this book are contributed to the Police Welfare Fund, as wished by him.

His love for creative writing prompted him to write a "shatakam" in Telugu on his favourite card game of 'Bridge', titled *Varadhi Shatakam* ('Varadhi' in Telugu means a bridge across a river or canal).

His last book *Idli in Paris,* a classic in English fiction published in 1996, just before his death, combines wit with insights into the devious methods employed by people in power. In the Introduction to this book, Vimala Anandaram, a litterateur of some repute herself, describes the author, Venugopal Rao as "a wordsmith in every sense of the term", adding that "The vignettes are laced with humour to make the overall picture less depressing. The readers will notice a 'Wodehousian tinge' in his writings."

In recognition of his enormous contribution to the field of Criminology and Criminal Justice Administration, Venugopal Rao was conferred the Kumarappa-Reckless Award in 1980, the highest honour awarded by the Indian Society of Criminology. This award has been conferred in different years on persons of eminence like Justice V.R. Krishna Iyer, Justice M.N. Venkatachalaiah, K.F. Rustamji, M.S. Gore, N.R. Madhava Menon, et al.

The crowning glory of his academic achievements came in 1993, in the form of award of the degree (*honoris causa*) of Doctor of Letters (D Litt) by the prestigious Andhra University. Vishakhapatnam for "no ordinary intellectual achievement in having authored eleven scholarly books in English, penned some well-researched monographs, directed research projects in a difficult and little explored field and published scores of articles, stories and plays in both English and Telugu". This has indeed been a rare and unparalleled honour bestowed on any police officer in the country.

Venugopal Rao was indeed a jewel in the crown of the Indian Police Service. A gifted police professional, an outstanding personality of towering intellect and great erudition, who particularly stands out for his sterling contribution of bringing academic focus to criminal justice administration in the country.

17

Kalyan Rudra

K.P. Singh

Born in Chittagong, Bangladesh, on May 10, 1938, to Padmini Bhushan Rudra (father) and Saroju Rudra (mother), Kalyan Rudra moved to Kolkata with his family prior to partition. He attended the prestigious St. Xavier's School in Kolkata and did his BSc and MSc in Mathematics from St. Xavier's College. After an initial foray with the Indian Forest Service, Kalyan Rudra joined the

Indian Police Service in 1960, Punjab being his first state cadre. He subsequently moved to Haryana.

Kalyan Rudra got married in 1966 to Mridula (Ray) Rudra and they were blessed with two sons. Their elder son, Kaushik, has pursued a career in banking abroad, whereas, the younger son, Rithwik, followed in the footsteps of his father and joined the IPS in 1993. Mr. Rudra was blessed with four granddaughters, two each through both of his sons. He used to absolutely dote on his four little granddaughters; showered them with love, affection and gifts at every opportunity. Mr. Rudra was a very devoted family man and he always loved to have the family around him. His second love, and some would say, his primary love was always his work. He was absolutely passionate about his work and lived and breathed it. He would come back home late from work, sit down in front of the TV, watching either the news or cricket, and continuing to do his office work. Cricket and to a lesser extent football were big sources of joy for him. His passion for cricket continued till the very end. We are told that even 24 hours before his death, he was discussing some "misfits" from the Bangladesh cricket team.

Kalyan Rudra is regarded as one of the best police officers Haryana ever received, so far as his professional skills, devotion to duty, integrity and commitment welfare of men he commanded were concerned.

After completing his training at PTS Phillaur, he remained posted as ASP in the districts of Patiala and Faridkot. He commanded the 25th Battalion of the Punjab Armed Police before joining ITBP on March 17, 1965. He serviced for two years in ITBP. After rejoining in Haryana, he got his first posting as District Superintendent of Police, Mahendergarh at Narnaul. Because of professional qualities and image of a strict disciplinarian, he was handpicked to head the district police Rohtak. Rohtak had been the most notorious and crime infested district of Haryana. Mr. Rudra grabbed the opportunity and by dint of his perseverance and professional qualities he earned a name for himself as a hard taskmaster and commander of the district for five years continuously. He eradicated the menace of dacoity, robbery and organized crime from the area. Cracking of the Pratap Singh Kairon murder case had been like a diamond in his professional career. Partap Singh Kairon was the sitting Chief Minister of Punjab and was assassinated on GT Road near Sonepat in district Rohtak. After that he became famous as a tough and brave police officer whose name was known to each and every Haryanvi household.

He also remained posted as SSP Hisar. His knowledge of crimes, criminals, police record and administrative affairs was unmatchable. Even today, young IPS officers are recommended to read his inspection reports and tour notes. He was a top performer and a hard taskmaster. He commanded the ranges of Ambala and Hisar as DIG and also headed the state intelligence agency for a brief period.

One of his admirers who is alive described him as an officer who was the messiah of poor and downtrodden people and who always listened to their grievances and ensured instant relief and justice to them. Haryanvis remember him with great respect and reverence. He was an embodiment of courtesy, courage, confidence and camaraderie.

After completing his field assignments with the Haryana Police as Superintendent of Police and Deputy Inspector General of Police, Mr. Rudra joined the Intelligence Bureau as Deputy Director on June 30, 1978. He served in the IB for thirteen long years, holding different assignments of sensitive nature, till June 25, 1991, when he was recalled by his home cadre state to head the Haryana Police. His colleagues in IB remember him as an officer who was thorough, meticulous, rule-oriented, caring and methodical. He believed in the planning of an operation till the last detail. He was a pioneer in undertaking counter terrorism operations in IB. He always gave due credit of success to his subordinates and, at times, went out of the way to reward them. His concerns for safety of his men during counter terrorist operations was beyond compare. He introduced the system of methodical reporting of incidents to the hierarchy amd was a man with a great heart.

It was his expertise in counter terrorism operations during his posting in IB that Mr. Rudra was specially called from deputation to head the Haryana Police at a time when the state was suffering from Sikh militancy as the Haryana Police was not adequately trained and equipped to meet the challenges. He exhibited extreme sense of devotion and professionalism and raised the Haryana

Police as a fighting unit to combat terrorism successfully. It was under his leadership and command that the Haryana Police could eradicate terrorism from the state. He served the Haryana Police as its DGP on two occasions from June 25, 1991 to August 17, 1994 and from November 3, 1995 to May 16, 1996. During this period he not only led the Haryana Police with grace but also trained and inspired the whole generation of IPS officers to meet future challenges. He also served with distinction as DG/RPF from August 18, 1994 to November 2, 1995. He was awarded the Police Medal for meritorious services in the year 1977 and the President's Police Medal for distinguished services in 1987.

As a person, Mr. Rudra was a role model for many young officers even today. He was blessed with a strong memory; his ability to remember names, dates, places and directions was unequalled and he could reel off names of villages along with associated incidents, almost at will. He put his strong memory and logical mind to good use by getting to know the people he worked with and the people he served; while this seemed like a small gesture, it made a major difference to people around him. It was an acknowledgement that he knew them and cared for them. This helped to forge a bond of friendship and connection; some of these continue till date, even though he had been dead for more than a decade. His son, Kaushik, told me that though he was a strict disciplinarian in his professional life, in his personal life, he had a sharp sense of humour. Like his younger brother, Dipak Rudra, with whom he shared a close bond, he loved regaling everyone with jokes. Mr. Rudra was a dog lover. He took a special liking to Zeus, a black Labrador. Zeus mourned for hours after Mr. Rudra died in 2005 and left to join him soon after.

Kalyan Rudra was very simple in his food habits. He loved a good meal like everyone else. Being a good Bengali, he was fond of prawns (chingri mach), cooked in the traditional Bengali way, with mustard oil. He developed a strong taste for food from Punjab and Haryana as well. He loved eating *Bajra Ki Roti* with *Sarson Da Saag* and topping off the meal with *Gur Shakkar*. At tea time, he would love eating *samosas*.

He took to writing books in a big way after his retirement and published four books, including *Rise and Fall of Punjab Terrorism*

(1978-1993), *New Security Challenges and Vulnerabilities* and *Global Terror*. While these dealt mostly with issues of militancy and security challenges, based on his first hand experience of these issues, he also wrote an account of his personal life, in a book titled *No Humdrum Life*.

The author had the privilege of serving under Mr. Rudra as District Superintendent of Police as well as in the capacity of his staff officer. He was indeed a through professional, lovable family man, perfect husband, adorable father, wonderful boss, generous commander, humanity personified and, above all, a pious soul. He was a rare officer who is remembered with reverence and respect by all, including subordinates, colleagues, peers and people in general. May God Almighty bless his soul with peace and *moksha* to him.

18

Shrawan Tandon

Prakash Singh

Shrawan Tandon was one of the finest police officers this country has produced. A man of tremendous integrity, indomitable will and unflinching determination, he was a role model for the police officers of his generation.

Born on November 24, 1922, he belonged to Farrukhabad district and started his career as a commissioned officer of the Indian Army in 1942. Later, in 1947, he was selected for the Indian Police

Service. After training, he was posted as Assistant Superintendent of Police, Moradabad. He also served as Superintendent of Police, Kumbh Mela, Allahabad. As District Superintendent of Police, he served in Etah, Rampur, Shahjahanpur and Faizabad districts. He was Senior Superintendent of Police of Varanasi and Kanpur districts. It was in these assignments that his reputation spread all over the state as a fair and just officer who stood no nonsense and brooked no interference from politicians.

After promotion, he served as DIG, Bareilly Range and thereafter went on deputation to the Centre. He was DIG Police, Delhi, where he dealt with the Central Government Employees' strike with great competence. He also served as IG, CRPF, Hyderabad. In all these assignments, he left his stamp as a strict officer who enforced discipline and maintained order even under the most adverse circumstances.

My first contact with Mr. Tandon was when he was Senior Superintendent of Police, Kanpur. After my training in PTC, Moradabad, I was posted as Assistant Superintendent of Police (Probationer) under him. I was forewarned that Tandon Sahib was a very strict officer. With a feeling of trepidation, I called on him. However, I found him very warm hearted and affectionate. In fact, he treated me as a member of the family. Mrs. Sarala Tandon was also a graceful and affectionate lady, qualities which she retains to this day. In fact, I used to look upon Mr. and Mrs. Shrawan Tandon as an ideal couple—made for each other.

Mr. Tandon would make me sit along with him in the office just to give me a feel of the responsibilities of a Senior Superintendent of Police. Merely being in his company was an education. His disposal of papers was fast. Visitors were heard with patience and their grievances sought to be redressed. Politicians were given due courtesy but they were not allowed to take liberties or influence the functioning of the police. During his tours and inspections also, Mr. Tandon would take me along. The station officers shuddered at the prospect of his impending inspection. They knew that he could not be pleased by sumptuous meals or in any other irregular manner. A thorough professional and a hard taskmaster, Mr. Tandon would inspect the various facets of police working in great detail.

Mr. Tandon's Friday parades at the police lines were an

unforgettable experience. He was very particular about attending the parades. The Reserve Inspector would ensure that all the staff was well turned out and that the drill was of a high standard. In view of his army background, Mr. Tandon was very particular about these points. He had a thundering voice and his commands would resonate all over the parade ground. The saying was that even the trees would be at 'Attention' while Mr. Tandon was on the parade ground. He would make it a point to go round the entire area of the police lines. Everything had to be spick and span.

Recruitment of constables has become such a messy affair these days. I cannot forget the selection process I saw in Kanpur in 1962. All the prospective candidates were lined up. Mr. Tandon moved in front of them, giving them a sharp look. All those he considered fit for recruitment were asked to take one step forward. The rest were screened out summarily. Those tentatively selected were of course subsequently measured and tested. No fingers were raised. No doubts were expressed. No motives were imputed. Everyone knew that the fittest had been chosen

On one occasion, when I was posted in Lucknow and had come to Kanpur to attend a function, Mr. and Mrs. Tandon insisted that we stay with them. Pankaj, my son, was a small child then (he is an IG today) and was very mischievous. My wife was apprehensive that Pankaj might damage or disturb things in the Tandons' meticulous household. She was quite tense at the prospect of having to stay in the SSP's house. Mr. and Mrs. Tandon however made us feel completely at home.

Following the revolt in the UP PAC in 1973, Mr. Tandon's services were requisitioned by the state. He was posted as IG PAC and entrusted with restoring order and discipline in the force. At this stage, I had also been repatriated to the state after a stint in the Intelligence Bureau. Mr. Tandon selected me as his AIG PAC. I had no background of armed police, but learnt that under Mr. Tandon's stewardship. Needless to say, PAC was brought back on the rails, thanks to Mr. Tandon's dynamic leadership. Mr. Tandon was later elevated as Director General of Police, UP. Here again, he chose me as his Assistant Inspector General. Working with him was stressful and yet it was a delightful experience for the simple reason that no extraneous considerations weighed with him and everything about him was straightforward and above board.

At the peak of his career, Mr. Tandon was Director General of the Border Security Force. His army background made him eminently suitable for the top assignment in the country's premier paramilitary force. He toured extensively in the different frontiers and struck a chord with the officers and jawans deployed in the forward areas. He was the only DG BSF who took the salute himself on the Raising Day Parade on December 1; his argument was that it was Raising Day of the Force and, as its Commander, it was his privilege to take the salute. He is remembered to this day as an officer who never minced his words, always forthright and looked after the welfare of the jawans. Officers of the BSF who served under him still recall their association with Mr. Tandon with a feeling of nostalgia.

Shrawan Tandon retired on November 30, 1980. He lived for another 27 years and died on December 16, 2007. Unfortunately, he did not enjoy good health in the last few months of his life. His legacy however lives on, though it is being carried forward by a much smaller percentage of officers.

19

Kumar Trishool Dhari Singh

Sanjay Sinha

Kumar Trishool Dhari Singh, a 1974 batch IPS officer of the Tripura part of Manipur-Tripura cadre, rose to become the Director General of Police, Tripura. He was an illustrious and, in many respects, a legendary figure of the Tripura Police who, by his talent, diligence and skilful leadership, brought name and fame for the Tripura Police in the country.

K.T.D. Singh was born on July 5, 1948 to Laal Muni Kunwar and Ramnath Singh at Moresarai village, now part of Rohtas District, of Bihar. He is remembered as a disciplined child who, being the eldest of four siblings, was always caring and responsible towards the family.

Singh studied in the Multipurpose High School in Sasaram. He was a brilliant student and had a good academic track record. Not surprisingly, he was a favourite of his teachers. He was admired by his schoolmates for his humility and amiable nature. He did his graduation in History (Honours) from Patna College and postgraduation in History from Patna University, clearing the examination in the first division.

Since his early childhood he dreamed of joining the civil services and sincerely pursued his goal. In 1971, he appeared for the civil services examination and qualified for the Himachal Pradesh Administrative Services. After three years, he appeared again for the civil services examination and qualified for the Indian Police Service in the 1974 batch. He was allotted to the Tripura part of the joint Manipur-Tripura cadre.

After his initial training in the state, he was first posted as the Asst. SP (West Tripura) in January 1976 and, thereafter, as SDPO (Kailashahar) in February 1977. During his tenure as SDPO, he showed glimpses of his potential as a professional police officer. He effectively controlled the law and order situation and crime in his sub-division with a firm hand. This led to his elevation as the SP of North Tripura district, of which Kailashahar sub-division is a part.

During June 1980, Tripura witnessed large-scale communal disturbances between tribals and non-tribals, mostly in two of the three Tripura districts, namely, South and West districts. These two districts were afflicted with communal riots in which hundreds of people lost their lives, thousands of houses were burnt and thousands of people were displaced. As SP of North Tripura district, which also witnessed its share of disturbances though not as much as in the remaining two districts of the state, Mr. Singh, by his skilful management firmly maintained total peace in his jurisdiction. His capable handling of the law and order situation and leadership in managing a divided police during the troubled days earned accolades from all sections of the society—both tribal and non-tribal.

After his successful stint as SP of North Tripura district, he was posted as SP of the much more disturbed West Tripura district in September 1980. During this tenure, he played a pivotal role in ensuring peace in the riot-torn district and bringing about a sense of safety and security among the people. His firm handling and prompt action to nip the problems in the bud helped him in restoring normalcy in the communally sensitive and politically volatile district.

Large-scale communal disturbances in the state between the tribals, the indigenous population of the state, on the one hand, and the more numerous non-tribals, mostly Bengali settlers, on the other, gradually gave rise to tribal insurgency in the state. The situation was compounded by the fact that Tripura is surrounded on three sides by Bangladesh, in parts of which, helped by porous border and similar ethnic dispensation, the tribal insurgents could easily take refuge.

After his deft handling of the riot-torn West Tripura district, Singh's next challenge was streamlining the intelligence gathering apparatus of the state. This he achieved during his posting as the SP of the Special Branch in May 1983. During this period, insurgency began gathering steam but was held in check by the effective intelligence network set up of the Special Branch which provided vital inputs in helping to curb insurgency to a large extent in the state.

Mr. Singh's outstanding performance in the field of gathering intelligence in Tripura was duly noticed and it helped him in earning a posting on central deputation to the Intelligence Bureau. He remained posted in IB from May 1985 to September 1997 during which he did assignments in Jammu & Kashmir and at several desks at the headquarters in New Delhi including that of the Counter-Intelligence.

Mr. Singh returned to Tripura on repatriation in October 1997 and was posted as ADG Intelligence. Meanwhile, insurgency in Tripura had reached its peak with the state registering the maximum number of killings of both civilians as well as members of the security forces. His effective approach helped in revitalizing the intelligence gathering machinery of the state and, thereby, bolstering the efforts of the Tripura Police and other Central Para Military Forces in countering the outlawed insurgent groups like NLFT, ATTF and several others in different parts of the state.

The state government, impressed with his performance, elevated Mr. Singh to the post of Director General of Police when he had not even completed 25 years of service in the IPS. He assumed charge of the DGP Tripura in April 1999 and graced that post up to May 2000 when he had to step down because of some technical problems pointed out by the MHA in his posting as the DGP.

During this short period at the helm of affairs of the Tripura Police, Singh set into motion steps which ultimately resulted in gradual weakening of the insurgent movement in the state. He worked towards modernization of the Tripura Police, which included, increasing the number of battalions of Tripura State Rifles, an armed police force of the state modelled on the CPMFs. Tripura State Rifles played a crucial role in rooting out insurgency from Tripura in the coming years.

Thereafter, he went back on central deputation and was posted as the Inspector General CRPF at New Delhi from September 2000 to May 2006 during which he, inter alia, handled the operational matters at the headquarters.

He returned to Tripura in August 2006 and was initially posted as the ADG (Intelligence) and then as the DGP (Home Guards & Fire Service). He formally became the DGP Tripura again in March 2007. Though the insurgency had already been controlled to a great extent by then, under his leadership a decisive push was given to root it out completely.

Tripura is relatively a small state and insurgency in the north-eastern states is not uncommon. However, what is remarkable about the rooting out of insurgency from Tripura is the fact that it has been achieved without the Tripura Police, spearheaded by the Tripura State Rifles, resorting to strong arm tactics. It is a fact which was duly recognized by the central government when the Tripura Police became only the fourth state police in the country to get the President's Colours in 2011. The credit obviously goes to the top police leadership of the state.

Singh was a police professional to his fingertips. Whatever he did, he did very efficiently, effectively and with single-mindedness. Once he had assessed a situation, he was very firm in resolving the issue and would not shy away from using force wherever necessary. In a state which is politically highly polarized, he was liked by both ends of the political spectrum which speaks a lot about his integrity, impartiality as well as his effectiveness as a police officer.

This Stalwart leader of the Tripura Police died on May 2, 2008 while on duty. In honour of his dedicated services to the State of Tripura in general and the Tripura Police in particular, the Tripura Police Training Academy has been renamed as K.T.D. Singh Police Training Academy by the Government of Tripura and his bust placed at the entrance point of the institution.

About the Contributors

M.K. Narayanan, former Director, Intelligence Bureau, and former National Security Advisor. He was also the Governor of West Bengal.

Julio Ribeiro, former Commissioner of Police, Mumbai, former DG of Police, Gujarat and Punjab. He was also India's Ambassador to Romania.

Sudershan Sharma, 1958 batch IPS Officer, served in Delhi Police, the BSF, the National Academy of Administration, ITDC and CISF. He was responsible for implementation of computer systems in para-military forces.

P.V. Rajgopal, former Director, SVP National Police Academy, Hyderabad, is the author of the bestselling two-volume biography of K.F. Rustamji.

Kalyan K. Mitra, former Director of Aviation Research Centre (ARC) and was the Principal Director, DG Security. He has authored many articles dealing with various strategic issues.

Ashok K. Abrol, belonging to West Bengal cadre, served as Special DG, Railway Protection Force. He had worked in different districts of West Bengal, Intelligence Branch of West Bengal Police, CISF and SSB in various capacities. He was awarded the Indian Police Medal for Meritorious Service and also the President's Police Medal for Distinguished Service.

A.P. Bhatnagar, former Director General of Police, Punjab, was Advisor to Justice J.S. Verma Commission of Enquiry (relating to former Prime Minister Rajiv Gandhi's death.)

Biswakesh Tripathy, a very senior IPS Officer of Orissa cadre. He served as IG in BSF and CRPF. Took voluntary retirement as IG, CRPF. He has authored 14 books in English and Oriya.

Amiya Bhushan Tripathy, 1962 batch IPS Officer of Odisha cadre. He retired as Director General of Police, Odisha in 1997. He has authored six books—two in English, including *Diaries of a Country Cousin: Policing the Nation*.

K.M. Singh, 1968 batch IPS Officer of Maharashtra cadre served in IB for three decades, former Director General of CISF and Member, National Disaster Management Authority (NDMA).

Sankar Sen, former Director, SVP National Police Academy, Hyderabad, and former Director General, National Human Rights Commission. Currently, he is the Senior Fellow (Human Rights) at the Institute of Social Sciences, New Delhi.

Chaman Lal, former DG of Nagaland. He was also the Special Rapporteur of the National Human Rights Commission. Recipient of Padma Shree Award and Nana Palkhiwala Award for civil liberties.

B.P. Saha, IPS Officer of Orissa cadre. He served in different assignments in CBI, BSF and the Railway Protection Force. He was a Fellow of the Indian Institute of Advanced Studies, Shimla, and a former Director of Maulana Abul Kalam Institute of Asian Studies.

D.N.S. Shrivastava, former Director General of Police, Assam, and has also worked as the Superintendent of Police and DIG of Police, Western Range, Assam. In Assam, he had worked with and under K.P.S. Gill.

K.K. Paul was the former Commissioner of Police, Delhi and former Governor of Manipur and Uttarakhand.

Kamal Kumar, former Director, SVP National Police Academy, was also the Director of the National Institute of Criminology and Forensic Science. He held the elected position of Vice Chairman, UN Commission on Crime Prevention & Criminal Justice, Vienna.

K.P. Singh, former Director General of Police, Haryana and presently heading the State Vigilance Bureau. He has authored a number of books on different subjects, including human rights, criminology, police training and victimology. He has also written some novels and story books.

Prakash Singh, former Director General of Police of Uttar Pradesh and Assam, was also the Director General of Border Security Force. He was awarded Padma Shri in 1991 in recognition of his contribution to national security. Currently, he is the Chairman of the Indian Police Foundation and a distinguished member of the Advisory Board of Vivekananda International Foundation.

Sanjay Sinha, an IPS officer of Manipur-Tripura cadre, served in Intelligence Bureau for a long stretch of time. He retired as Director General of Police, Tripura.